Preserving and Pickling

Contents

3

CONTENTS

CONTENTS

Preserving and Pickling

I

Some General Directions

CHAPTER I

SOME GENERAL DIRECTIONS

EVERY housekeeper knows what a comfort it is to have a good supply of her own preserves and pickles which she can rely upon when the winter season comes around, and fresh fruits are hard to obtain or are too expensive. The putting up of one's own preserves and pickles is fascinating work, and it is surprising how quickly the pantry shelves may be filled with these delicacies by doing up a small quantity of fruit at a time, and the expense is scarcely felt at all.

The housewife need not be afraid of her preserves and pickles spoiling if she follows the few simple directions given here.

THE PROPER UTENSILS

By using the proper utensils the preserving of fruits and pickles may be greatly lightened.

13

First in importance are the kettles, which should always be either of granite, porcelain-lined or earthenware. Never use tin, iron or aluminum ware. Nearly all fruits contain more or less acid, and the above named materials will be affected by it. For the same reason use silver, wooden or porcelain-lined spoons for stirring or lifting the fruits. Wooden spoons are fine for stirring the hot fruits over the fire, since wood is a poor conductor, and the handle does not get so unbearably hot as with silver.

Other utensils needed will be coarse and fine strainers, enameled colander, enameled long-handled dippers, enameled fruit funnels; sharp knives for the peeling of fruits, and a pair of scissors which will be quite useful for snipping stems, and so forth. Measuring cups and spoons are quite essential for measuring the juice, etc.

You must have good kitchen scales, since it will be necessary to weigh the fruit and sugar if you are to get the right proportions. A food chopper is also very useful, since it may be used

in chopping vegetables when making relishes, cat-
sups and such things, and also in making some
kinds of preserves and marmalades. Then a
cherry-stoner, a strawberry huller, a raisin or
grape seeder, a pineapple corer and eye clip, and
a fruit press, although they are not absolutely
necessary, are very convenient to have, and make
the work much lighter. If you are preserving on
a large scale they are indispensable.

Of course there are the glasses and jars for
storing the fruit, necessary bowls to hold the
juice in straining, jelly bags and holders, and jar-
holders, to make it pleasanter to handle the hot jars.

The Sterilization of Glasses and Jars

Complete sterilization of the glasses and jars,
and also the utensils used is necessary if your
fruit is to keep perfectly. This is done by im-
mersing the glasses and jars in hot water, or
better still, placing them in cold water in a vessel
and bringing the water to the boiling point. A
little baking soda added to the water will aid in

this sterilization.   Keep the glasses and jars filled with boiling water or immersed in boiling water until you are ready to fill them.   Don't forget that what is necessary for the jars is also necessary for the lids.

Always fill the glasses or jars to overflowing, and place on the lids while hot.   The rubbers should be dipped in boiling water before using. When screw top glasses or jars are not used cover the top of preserves, jellies, jams and marmalades with melted paraffin before putting on the lids. In these cases do not fill the glasses quite to the top, but allow room for the paraffin.

Cans should be perfect, and rubbers new. Nearly all the failures in preserving and pickling come either from incomplete sterilization of utensils, careless handling, or an insufficient amount of heat, or because the jars are not sealed properly.

The Materials

Unless the materials used are good you cannot expect perfect results.   Discard all imperfect and overripe fruits, and the vegetables used should be up to standard. In spicing and pickling fruits and vegetables use only the best cider vinegar. If too strong it is better to weaken it with water than to buy weak vinegar, which always lacks in flavor. Whole spices are better than the ground spices, as they retain their strength longer. If ground spice is used it should be freshly ground. There is quite an art in combining different fruits so as to get a variety. This also often means quite a saving, since cheaper fruits may be combined with some of the more expensive kinds with the most satisfactory results.

II

Preserves and Conserves

CHAPTER II

PRESERVES AND CONSERVES

THE secret of making good preserves is to keep the fruit as whole and as clear as possible. The syrup should be rather thick before the fruit is added, and then the fruit simmered very slowly in this until clear and transparent; then it should be lifted carefully with a strainer into the glasses or jars. The syrup should be boiled to the consistency of jelly before being poured over the fruit.

PLUM PRESERVES

The yellow or green-gage plums, or the red plums are good for preserves, although any kind may be used. Scald the plums with boiling water, and remove the skin. Halve, and seed. Weigh the fruit and allow a pound of sugar to each pound of fruit. Place the fruit in a preserving kettle, then let it stand overnight. In the morning pour off the juice and boil to a syrup, then add the fruit, and simmer very slowly until clear. Lift the plums carefully out with a strainer and fill into glasses or jars; then when the syrup has been boiled to the consistency of jelly pour over the fruit, and seal up while hot.

PEACH PRESERVES

Use large yellow peaches for these preserves, peel, and quarter. If you wish the skins may be removed by pouring boiling water over them. Place the peaches in a preserving kettle and to each pound of fruit use three-fourths of a pound of sugar. Let them stand overnight, then in the morning pour off the syrup, and boil to a thick honey. Add the fruit and simmer slowly until transparent, then lift with strainer into glasses or jars, and seal.

APPLE PRESERVES

Use good large tart apples for preserves, peel, core and quarter. To each pound of fruit add one pound of sugar and one cupful of water. Place the water and sugar in a preserving kettle with the juice and yellow rind of one or two oranges or lemons, and a stick of cinnamon. Boil to a syrup; then add the apples and cook slowly until transparent. The apples should be ripe and tender, but as whole as possible. Fill into glasses or jars and seal.

WATERMELON PRESERVES

Divide a watermelon in quarters, and trim away the green outside rind, also remove all the red inside part. Cut the white part into small pieces, either cubes or strips, and cover with a weak brine and let stand overnight. Drain and rinse, and boil in water until the rind is tender enough to be easily pierced with a fork. Make a syrup with water and sugar, allowing one pound of sugar to each pound of melon, also one thinly-sliced lemon to each pound of fruit, and one-half teaspoonful ground ginger root. Boil the syrup until thick, and add the fruit, and simmer slowly until transparent. Fill into jars, pour over syrup and seal.

Currant Preserves

Use the large red currants for this preserve. Arrange in alternate layers in a preserving kettle with sugar, using a pound of sugar for each pound of fruit. Let stand several hours, then pour off the juice, and boil to a thick syrup; then add the currants, and cook several minutes longer, or until the syrup jellies when tested. Fill into glasses or jars, and seal.

Currant Conserve

To a quart of currant juice prepared as for jelly add two quarts of red currants, two pounds of raisins chopped and seeded, the juice and grated rind of a half dozen oranges, and six pounds of sugar. Boil until thick, stirring constantly. Put into glasses and seal.

Quince Preserves

In making this preserve use two-thirds quinces, and one-third sweet or semi-sweet apples. Pare and quarter the fruit, and core, removing all hard parts; then slice into thin slices. Cover the quinces with cold water and simmer until tender, then remove with a strainer, and add the sweet apples to the water that remains, adding a little more water if necessary. Cook the apples until tender, then remove with a strainer.

Boil the juice for several minutes before adding the sugar. Allow three-quarters of a pound of sugar to each pound of fruit. After the sugar is in, boil until the syrup is thick, then add the fruit, and cook until clear and of the right consistency for preserves. The fruit should not be stirred, but kept as unbroken as possible. Fill into preserve jars and seal. This makes a delicious preserve.

Pear Preserves

Use carefully selected large pears, peel, quarter, and core; then cut up into eighths. To each seven pounds of the fruit use six pounds of granulated sugar, three lemons, and several pieces of green ginger root. Place the pears and sugar in alternating layers in a preserving kettle, and let stand overnight. In the morning place in the oven long enough to melt all the sugar, and pour off; then add to the juice all the grated yellow rind of the lemons, and the bits of ginger root. When boiled to a thick syrup remove the ginger root, and add the pears, and simmer slowly until transparent, and a golden color. Fill into jars. Boil the syrup down a little more, and pour over the fruit.

Apricot Preserves

To each seven pounds of preserved fruit use seven pounds of sugar, and the juice of one-half dozen oranges. Place the apricots and sugar together in a kettle and let stand overnight. In the morning drain off the syrup, and add the orange juice, and the grated rind of two of the oranges; and also a few of the blanched kernels of the stone, and bring to a boil; then add the fruit and simmer until the fruit is clear. Remove the fruit, and place in jars. Boil the syrup down until thick, and pour over.

CHERRY PRESERVES

Excellent cherry preserves can be made by taking the cherries after they have been soaked, and cover them with sugar, using equal parts of sugar and cherries. Let stand several hours; strain off the juice into a preserving kettle. Bring to a boil, then add the cherries and cook five minutes. Fill the cherries into preserve jars, boil the syrup until it is thick and ready to jelly, then pour over the fruit.

RED RASPBERRY PRESERVES

Red raspberries can be preserved in the same way as strawberries and are excellent combined with currants. Raspberry marmalade with currant juice is made by taking four quarts of red raspberries and one quart of ripe currants. Place raspberries in a preserving kettle, mash currants and extract the juice and add to the raspberries. Simmer slowly a half hour, then add an equal quantity of sugar, heating it in the oven before adding. Boil ten minutes, or until you have a thick preserve, and pour into jars.

GOOSEBERRY PRESERVES

The best way to make gooseberry preserves is to make a rich syrup with sugar and a little water. Add the berries (which should not be ripe), and let them remain for about ten or fifteen minutes, then skim out with a wire strainer, and put into preserve jars. Boil the syrup until it jellies, then pour over the fruit, and seal.

GOOSEBERRY-PINEAPPLE PRESERVES

A delicious preserve can be made by combining gooseberries and pineapple. Use one part of pineapple to two parts of gooseberries, or half and half as liked. Use one pound of sugar to each pound of fruit, and make as other preserves.

WHOLE PRESERVED STRAWBERRIES

Here are two excellent ways in which strawberries may be preserved whole :

Remove hulls from four pounds of nice, large, ripe berries, put them in a colander, rinse off with cold water, drain and place on platters. Cover with sugar, using one pound of sugar to each pound of fruit. Let the fruit stand overnight, and in the morning pour off the juice into a preserving kettle, and if all the juice has not melted, place the platters in the open a few moments.

Boil the juice, and measure, and to each two cups of strawberry juice add one cupful of currant juice that has been prepared as for jelly. Boil this until it jellies, then drop in the whole strawberries, and allow them to remain until thoroughly heated through. Put the berries into the preserve jars and pour the thick juice over. When cool pour melted paraffin on top, or seal up, according to the kind of jars used. This preserve keeps splendidly, and yet it is not too strong to be good.

Another method of preserving the berries whole is to make a "strawberry sunshine," by mashing some strawberries and adding to each pint of the pulp the same amount of sugar. Place this in a preserving kettle and boil slowly, until clear and thick. Pour the glasses about one-third full of this "sunshine," then place in these glasses after they have become heated nicely, firm, ripe berries, and fill up with the "sunshine." Place the jars on boards in the oven for several minutes, or long enough to insure the berries being heated through. When cool cover with melted paraffin and then with the lids. If preferred, the berries may be put down in sugar the night before, and the juice added to the pulp. This will make a stronger preserve.

STRAWBERRY-RED RASPBERRY PRESERVES

The red fruits may be nicely combined. A delicious preserve is made by taking equal parts of strawberries and red raspberries, and covering with granulated sugar, using a pound of sugar to each pound of fruit; let stand overnight. In the morning pour the juice into a preserving kettle; if sugar is not melted place in the oven a few moments. To each pint of this juice add one cup of currant juice.   Boil until a drop from a spoon will retain its shape when dropped on to a cold plate. Add the berries and boil about three minutes after the fruit has first come to a boil.   Fill into jars and seal.

TOMATO PRESERVES

Many people are fond of tomato preserves.   To make them, take four pounds of yellow pear tomatoes and three pounds of granulated sugar. Let stand overnight, then pour off all the juice and put into a preserving kettle.   Boil up into a thick syrup, clearing it with the white of an egg if necessary.   Then add the tomatoes, also two lemons, cut into thin slices, and a little ginger root.   Cook until the tomatoes are clear and the syrup thick.

SUN-PRESERVED CURRANTS

Currants are good sun-preserved.   For this purpose use only the most perfect berries, pick over carefully and wash.   The large cherry currants are best preserved in this manner.   Use two-thirds of a pound of sugar to each pound of fruit. Spread the currants on platters, and cover with sugar, and allow to stand overnight; then in the morning place the platters in the oven a few minutes to melt the sugar and extract the juice not brought out by the sugar.

Then place the platters in the sun in the hottest place you can find; they should be placed on light tables or stands so that they can be easily moved about as the sun changes. Cover with double mosquito netting to keep out the flies and other insects, placing something higher around the platters to keep the netting from getting down into the fruit. In two or three days the syrup about them will thicken up, and the fruit become semi-transparent. The time will depend on the intensity of the sun.

They are now ready to pack away in jars. Self-sealing jars are excellent for this purpose. Place some granulated sugar over the top, then pour over this melted paraffin and screw on the lids.

RHUBARB CONSERVE

To each three pounds of rhubarb, cut up into bits, add one-half pound of raisins, one-fourth pound of chopped almonds or English walnut meats, two lemons, and one cupful of pineapple. Seed and chop the raisins, slice the lemons very thin, and cut up the pineapple into small bits. Add enough water to start the juice flowing in the rhubarb, then add four pounds of sugar. Cook to a rich conserve, and fill glasses and seal up.

BARBERRY CONSERVE

Pick over and wash the berries, place in a preserving kettle and add enough water to about cover. Boil until the skins break, then press out all the juice. Add to this juice large seeded raisins, using about a pound of raisins to a cupful of the barberry juice, and a cupful of sugar. Boil to a thick conserve and fill glasses or jars.

GRAPE CONSERVE

To each pound of grapes that have been skinned, add the juice and grated rind of one orange, one-half pound of raisins, one-half pound of walnut meats, and one pound of sugar. If you wish a little lemon may also be added. Boil until thick and fill glasses or jars.

PINEAPPLE CONSERVE

Peel, eye, and core the pineapple, cut into bits and run through a food chopper, or grate as desired. To each pint of the pineapple pulp add one pint of rhubarb cut up into bits. Boil until tender, then add to each pint of fruit a pound of sugar, the juice and grated rind of three oranges and one cupful of almonds or English walnut meats chopped into bits. Boil to the consistency of a conserve, and fill into glasses. The orange rind may be omitted if you do not care for the orange flavor.

PLUM CONSERVE

Use damson or prune plums for this conserve. To each pound of plums use one-half pound of peaches and one-half pound of apricots, and one-half pound of seeded raisins. Cook the fruit together until soft, then add the sugar, using a pound of sugar to each pound of fruit. Cook to the consistency of a thick conserve. If you wish nut meats may be added or the kernels of the peach pits may be pounded to a paste and stirred in.

III

New Preserves From Combined Fruits

CHAPTER III

NEW PRESERVES FROM COMBINED FRUITS

THE housewife may have quite a variety of delicious preserves by combining different fruits. Inexpensive fruits can often be used with those that cost much more without detracting from the deliciousness of the preserves, and thereby the expense can be reduced. For instance, Siberian crab-apples combined with certain fruits, such as quinces, pears or plums, will make what most people consider a better preserve than when the fruit is used alone. Plums when used alone in preserves are very strong, and many people object to plum preserves on this account. If crab-apples are added, the result is a much milder preserve. The pear is counted by many as an insipid fruit, but when combined with other fruits the flavor is much improved.

Rhubarb is usually very cheap, especially in the latter part of the season, and can be combined with different fruits to advantage. In combining different fruits for preserves one should be careful to select those the flavors of which combine perfectly. We give here a number of recipes that have been tested and proved satisfactory. The housewife by experimenting may add many more kinds to her list.

To test for consistency of preserves or jelly, drop a small quantity of the mixture on a cold saucer. If it holds its shape it has been sufficiently cooked.

PLUM-CRAB-APPLE PRESERVES

In making this preserve use an equal quantity of Siberian crab-apples and plums—red plums, if possible, although any kind may be used. Wash the fruit and remove the stem and blossom ends, but do not peel, although all the black spots and knots should be removed. Cover the crab-apples with a little water and stew slowly until they are soft enough to press through a sieve. Cook the plums in another vessel until tender, adding just enough water to start the juice flowing, and pass through a sieve.

Stir the two kinds of pulp together and measure, allowing a pound of sugar to each pint of pulp. Bring the pulp to a boil and add the sugar after the latter has been heated in the oven. Continue to boil slowly until a thick preserve is obtained, stirring constantly. Fill into preserve jars and seal.

If red plums and red crab-apples are used, the result will be a rich red preserve. A green preserve is made by combining Greening apples with green-gage plums, and a yellow preserve with yellow-fleshed apples and yellow-gage or honey plums. If honey plums are used, do not use quite so much sugar, as they do not cook tart like other plums, but with a sweet, honey-like juice around them.

PINEAPPLE-RHUBARB PRESERVES

To each pound of cut-up rhubarb add one medium-sized pineapple and a pound and a half

of sugar.   Arrange the fruit and sugar in alternate layers in a preserving kettle, and let stand two
hours.   Put over the fire and slowly simmer to the
consistency of preserves. Fill preserve jars and seal.

PEAR-CRANBERRY PRESERVES

To each two pounds of pears use a pound of
cranberries, and a pound of sugar to each pound
of fruit.   Place the cranberries in a preserving
kettle and cover with water, using a quart of
water to each pound of fruit.   Stew until tender,
then pass through a sieve.   Pare, core and quarter medium-sized pears and weigh.   Add the
sugar to the cranberry juice and boil to a rather
thick syrup, then add the pears.   Let the mixture
simmer until tender and of a uniform color, then
fill into preserve jars with a strainer.   Let the
syrup boil until it begins to jelly; pour over the
fruit and seal.

PEAR-GRAPE PRESERVES

Use an equal quantity of grapes and pears.
Peel, quarter and core the pears, and stew in a

little water until tender, and pass through a coarse sieve. Stew the grapes until soft and pass through sieve. Mix the pulps together and measure. To each pint of pulp add three-fourths of a pound of sugar. Cook slowly until of the consistency of preserves, and fill jars.

BLACKBERRY-RHUBARB PRESERVES

To equal quantities of blackberries and rhubarb add a pound of sugar to each pound of fruit. Place the rhubarb in a preserving kettle with just enough water to start the juice flowing. When the rhubarb is tender add the sugar and let boil; add the blackberries and simmer slowly until of the right consistency for preserves or jam. Fill glasses and seal.

GOOSEBERRY-BLUEBERRY PRESERVES

To each two quarts of blueberries take one quart of gooseberries. Place the berries in a preserving kettle with a little water, and stew until tender; then add sugar that has been heated in the oven, adding a pound of sugar to each pound of fruit, and stew until of the right consistency for preserves or jelly. Fill glasses, and seal.

CURRANT-GOOSEBERRY PRESERVES

To a gallon of gooseberries use one quart of red-currant juice prepared as for jelly, and six pounds of sugar. Make a syrup with the currant juice and the sugar; then add the gooseberries that have been stemmed and tailed. Simmer slowly until the berries are a pretty clear red color, then fill into glass jars. Boil the juice down to the jelly stage, pour over the fruit, and seal.

BAR-LE-DUC CURRANTS AND GOOSEBERRIES

Take an equal quantity of currants and gooseberries, and to each pound of the fruit allow an equal quantity of sugar. Add just enough water to the sugar to dissolve nicely, and boil to the consistency of honey; then add the currants and gooseberries and boil the juice to a thick jelly-like syrup, or until it coats the skimmer; pour into jelly-glasses or pint jars, and seal. Either currants or gooseberries may be used alone.

GOOSEBERRY-PINEAPPLE PRESERVES

Use one medium-sized pineapple to each two quarts of gooseberries, and about four pounds of sugar. Carefully prepare the fruit. Add enough water to dissolve the sugar, boil to the consistency of honey, add the fruits and simmer slowly for several minutes. Boil the syrup until it thickens, and pour over the fruit. Pour the fruit into jars, and seal.

PINEAPPLE-APPLE PRESERVES

To one quart of tart apples peeled and cored, and cut up into cubes, add one quart of pineapple, peeled, cored and cut up into cubes. Place in a preserving kettle with two pounds of granulated sugar, one cupful of water, add the apples, and stew until nearly tender; then add the pineapple. Simmer until transparent, then with a skimmer

remove the fruit and fill into preserve jars. Boil
the syrup down to the jelly stage, and pour over
the preserves. Seal while hot.

GOOSEBERRY-RED RASPBERRY PRESERVES

Gooseberries and red raspberries in equal parts
make fine preserves. For this combination, use
one pound of sugar to each pound of fruit, as the
gooseberries are tart. In combining raspberries
and rhubarb, use two parts raspberries and one
part rhubarb for jam or jelly.

PEACH-RHUBARB PRESERVES

Use one pound of rhubarb to each two pounds
of peaches. The preserve will be better if only
the tender ends of the rhubarb are used. Peel
and quarter the peaches, and peel and cut up the
rhubarb in inch lengths. Place in a preserving
kettle with just enough water to start the juice
flowing, and simmer slowly until the fruit is
tender; then add the sugar after it has been
heated in the oven, using a pound of sugar to

each pound of fruit. Boil to the right consistency for preserves.

If you wish to keep the fruits whole, make a syrup with sugar and water, and boil down to a thick syrup. Add enough currant juice to make it a pretty pink color. Then add the peaches and rhubarb, a small quantity at a time, and boil just long enough in the syrup to cook thoroughly. Fill into the preserve jars with a strainer or spoon. Cook the juice until it begins to jelly, and pour over the fruit in the jars.

This makes a pretty as well as delicious preserve. If you do not have the currant juice, cranberry juice can be used, or a glass of currant jelly. Pears and rhubarb may be combined in the same manner.

Quince-Cranberry Preserves

Peel, core and cut into eighths some nice large quinces. Peel, core and quarter an equal quantity of sweet apples. Arrange the fruit in alternate layers in a preserving kettle with sugar, using to

each seven pounds of fruit five pounds of sugar.
Let stand overnight, and in the morning add one
quart of cranberry juice to each seven pounds of
fruit. Simmer slowly until the fruit is tender
and a pretty pink color throughout; then fill into
jars or glasses. Boil the syrup down to the consistency of jelly, pour over the fruit, and seal.

Tutti-Frutti Conserve

To make this conserve take an equal quantity
of white peaches, shredded pineapple, pears, rhubarb, tart apples and quinces. Green-gage plums
may also be used. Add to each pound of fruit
three-fourths of a pound of sugar. Cook until
the fruits are clear. Just enough water should be
added to start the fruit juices to flowing when the
sugar is added. Remove from the fire, and add
one-half pound of citron cut up into bits, and one
cupful of preserved ginger, and a half pound of
candied orange or lemon peel. If preferred, a
pound of English walnuts chopped may be added,
bringing to the boil again, and filling into jars.

This conserve is very much improved by adding the citron and candied peels. This is nice to make when you have small quantities of different kinds of fruit on hand, but not enough of any one kind to make up by itself.

TUTTI-FRUTTI PRESERVES

Use equal quantities of red raspberries, blackberries, peaches, rhubarb, pineapple and Siberian crab-apples, and allow one pound of sugar to each pound of fruit. Peel and quarter the peaches; peel, quarter and core the crab-apples; peel and cut the rhubarb in inch lengths and peel and shred the pineapple.

Place the fruits in a preserving kettle with a little water and simmer slowly until all the fruits are cooked; then add the sugar and stew until thick and clear, and fill into preserve jars.

QUINCE-APPLE PRESERVES

To each two pounds of quinces use one pound of sweet apples. Pare and quarter the fruit, removing all hard parts, then cut into thin slices. Cover the quinces with cold water and simmer until tender, then remove with a strainer.

Cook the sweet apples in the water that remains, adding more water if necessary to cover the apples. When tender remove with a strainer. Add the sugar to the juice in the kettle, using three-fourths of a pound of sugar to each pound of fruit. Boil until the syrup is thick, then add the fruit. Heat thoroughly, remove with a strainer and fill into jars. Boil the syrup until it is ready to jelly; pour over the fruit and seal.

Peach-Pineapple Preserves

To make these preserves use an equal quantity of ripe peaches and ripe pineapple. White peaches are the best for this preserve. To each pound of fruit add a pound of sugar. Boil to a thick preserve and fill into glasses or jars and seal up. The pineapple should be cut up into bits before adding to the peaches.

PINEAPPLE-GRAPEFRUIT PRESERVES

To make this preserve take three large grapefruits and one large pineapple. Peel, slice and core the pineapple and cut up into eighths. Cut the grapefruits into quarters and remove the fiber and seeds from the centers. Cut up the pulp in small bits. To each cupful of the combined fruits add one cupful of granulated sugar, and a bit of orange or lemon rind. Simmer slowly until the consistency of preserves, fill into glasses or jars and seal.

PEAR-LEMON PRESERVES

Slice the lemons thin and remove the seeds. Allow three pints of water to each pound of the fruit, and allow to stand overnight in this, then in the morning boil until tender. To each pint of this boiled fruit add one pint of sliced pears and one pound of granulated sugar. Boil until the pears are tender, and the syrup begins to jelly, and the fruit is transparent, then pour into jars and seal.

Pear Conserve

To each quart of peeled, cored and sliced pears use a cupful of maple sugar or syrup, one cupful of chopped and seeded raisins, the juice of two lemons, and the grated rind of one, and one cupful of English walnut meats, and two cupfuls of water. Boil until thick and fill into jars and seal.

Cherry-Strawberry Preserves

Use an equal quantity of red cherries and strawberries. Wash and stem the strawberries. Stem and stone the cherries. To each pound of the fruit use a pound of granulated sugar, and arrange in alternate layers with the fruit in a preserving kettle. Let the fruit stand overnight, then in the morning drain off the juice into a preserving kettle. Boil to a thick syrup, then add the fruit. Cook slowly until clear and transparent. Fill glasses or jars, and seal while hot.

Strawberry-Pineapple Preserves

To each quart of strawberries add one pint of pineapple cut up into cubes. To each pound of

the fruit use one pound of sugar. Arrange the
sugar and strawberries in alternate layers in a
preserving kettle, and let stand overnight.   In the
morning pour off the juice, and boil up, then add
the pineapple. Cook until the syrup begins to
thicken, then add the strawberries, and cook until
they are clear and transparent. Fill glasses or
jars and seal.

IV
Jellies and Jams

CHAPTER IV

JELLIES AND JAMS

QUIVERING, tempting, fine-flavored jelly is not in the least difficult to make if one knows just how to go about it. A jelly with a delicate natural flavor is much to be preferred to the strong jelly in which the natural fruit flavor has been destroyed in the making.

SELECTING THE FRUIT

In the first place great care should be taken in selecting the fruit. Some people have an idea that any sort of inferior fruit will do for jelly, but this is a mistake. Never use fruit for jelly that is overripe, for it not only requires more boiling to make it jelly, but it will also be much darker. Pectin, the substance in fruit that causes it to jelly, is at its best in fruits partly ripe or in their

57

prime. Gooseberries, grapes, currants, elderberries, strawberries, blackberries, raspberries, and
such like fruits will jelly best when only partially
ripe; while peaches, pears, quinces, apricots and
such like fruits will be best when perfectly ripe,
but not overripe.

Preparing the Fruit

All fruits should be carefully picked over and
washed, and all the fuzz on peaches and quinces
rubbed off. It is best to cook with their skins on
fruits intended for jelly, as it will give the jelly a
better flavor. Do not add water to currants or
any of the juicy fruits, but set over a very slow
fire until the juice begins to flow, then simmer
slowly until the fruit is tender. Fill the fruit in
a jelly bag and allow to drip into a vessel, but do
not squeeze with the hands if you wish to have a
nice clear jelly. After all the juice has dripped
out, then one may place the fruit in a fruit press
and squeeze out all the pulp possible. This can be
made up into jams.

PECTIN

Many fruits do not contain enough pectin or enough of acid to make them jelly quickly. In these cases it is a good idea to combine with them fruits that contain plenty of this necessary element of pectin and acid. Apples, crab-apples, currants, grapes and quinces are all excellent for this purpose. Currants are especially good to combine with the red fruits, such as strawberries, red raspberries and cherries. Apples are excellent to use when you do not wish to destroy the flavor of the other fruit used, since they are mild in flavor. Rhubarb, lemon, currants, gooseberries and cranberry juice will provide necessary acid for those fruits that are lacking in this quality.

SUGAR

The amount of sugar used should depend on the amount of pectin and acid the fruits contain. As a rule from three-fourths to a pound of sugar is used for each pint of juice. If a sour jelly is desired, of course, not so much sugar should be

used as for a sweet jelly.   Measure the juice, put
into a granite or porcelain-lined kettle and boil
for fifteen or twenty minutes, or more according
to the amount of water that has been added, and
the desired strength of the jelly.   In the mean-
time place the sugar in the oven, and heat until
hot, but not until it browns.   After putting in
the sugar it should be ready to take off in from
five to ten minutes; but one should always test
jelly by dropping some on a cold saucer or plate.
If it does not jelly right never make the mistake
of boiling it over again.   If you do this you will
have a thick, muddy, stringy compound, which is
far from the clear, tender yet firm, quivering
jelly which should be the result of your work.
The best way to do if the juice refuses to
jelly properly is to add to it more water, and
more fruit, and boil to a thick marmalade or
butter.

Fill your jelly into hot glasses or jars that have
been thoroughly sterilized.   Cover with melted
paraffin before placing on the lids.   Nowadays

one may obtain screw top glasses and jars that are not much more expensive than the ones with plain lids, and the jelly is more likely to keep in these, since they can be sealed tight.

Jams only differ from jelly in the fact that the pulp of the fruit is used, as well as the juices, the fruit being put through a sieve or fruit press.

APPLE MINT JELLY

For this jelly use nice tart, summer or winter apples, wash and cut up into bits. Add enough water to cover, and let simmer slowly until tender; then crush and fill into jelly bag and allow to drain into a vessel. Place the juice thus obtained in a preserving kettle, measuring it as you do so. Tie a bunch of fresh mint with a string, hang it in the juice, and let it simmer there for twenty or thirty minutes, then remove the mint, adding the hot sugar. Use three-fourths of a pound of sugar to each pint of juice. Boil to the consistency of jelly, and fill glasses.

QUINCE-ORANGE JELLY

Use the peel, but not the cores of quinces in making this jelly. Cut up into bits and simmer in a little water until tender. Drain off the juice, then add an equal quantity of orange juice, and a little bit of the thin yellow rind. Simmer for fifteen or twenty minutes; then add the sugar, using three-fourths of a pound of sugar to each pint of juice. Boil to the consistency of jelly, and fill into glasses and seal.

BARBERRY-APPLE JELLY

Use an equal quantity of apples and barberries, boiling them separately. Drain off the juice, and to each pint add one pound of sugar. Boil for fifteen or twenty minutes, add the hot sugar, and cook to the consistency of jelly.

CHERRY-CURRANT JELLY

To each pint of cherry juice add one cupful of currant juice. Mash the fruit with a wooden spoon, and drain off the juice into a preserving kettle. Boil fifteen to twenty minutes, add the hot sugar, boil to the consistency of jelly, and pour into glasses.

PLUM-CRAB-APPLE JELLY

If you wish a good pink jelly use the red-cheeked crab-apples, and red plums, but if you prefer a green jelly, use green crab-apples and green-gage plums. Wash the crabs, and cut out any bad specks, but leave whole and with the skins on. Add the plums and enough water to partly cover. Boil until soft, mash with a wooden spoon, fill into jelly bag and drain off juice. Proceed as in making other jelly. You can use an equal quantity of each fruit, or if you wish the plum taste to predominate, then use one-fourth as much crabs as plums.

ORANGE-LEMON JELLY

To each dozen of oranges use one-half dozen of lemons. Peel the yellow rind of half of the oranges and the lemons, being very careful not to get any of the bitter white pith. To each pound of sugar use one-half cupful of water. Place together in a preserving kettle with the thin rind, and simmer slowly for fifteen or twenty minutes; then strain and add the orange and lemon juice. Boil to the consistency of jelly, and fill glasses.

CRANBERRY-PEAR JELLY

Pears do not contain enough of pectin to make a good jelly when used alone. Cranberry or currant juice is excellent to use with the pear juice. Use an equal quantity of each kind of juice, and three-fourths of a pound of sugar to each pint of juice. Boil to the consistency of jelly and fill the glasses.

PEACH-RHUBARB JELLY

White peaches are best for jelly. Rub the fuzz from the peaches, and place in a preserving kettle. Use just enough water to start the juice to flowing, and simmer until tender. Crush with a wooden spoon, and fill into jelly bag, and let drain into vessel. To each pint of juice add one cupful of rhubarb juice, and allow three-fourths of a pound of sugar to each pint of juice. Proceed in the usual manner.

PINEAPPLE-APPLE JELLY

In making pineapple jelly the eyes and cores may be used. Cut the pineapple up into bits, and add enough water to nearly cover, and cook until tender. To each pint of the pineapple juice add one cupful of apple juice, and one pound of sugar. Proceed as in making other jelly.

SPICED GRAPE JELLY

Use green grapes or partly green grapes for this. Add to the grapes some stick cinnamon, a few cloves and bits of mace, and about an ounce of each to each six pounds of grapes. Boil until the juice flows freely. Drain off the juice. Add three-fourths of a pound of sugar to each pint of the spiced juice, and proceed as in making other jelly. This is good to serve with meats.

Pineapple-Orange Jelly

To each cupful of pineapple juice add a cupful of orange juice, and the juice of one lemon, and a bit of the rind. Boil for fifteen or twenty minutes, add the hot sugar, using a pound to each pint of juice; boil to the consistency of jelly, and fill jars.

Quince Jelly

This jelly may be made by using the parings of both the quinces and apples that were used in making preserves with a little more of the whole fruit added. Cut up the quinces and apples that are to be used, and add to the parings, then cover with water and simmer very slowly until the fruit is tender. Fill into a jelly bag, and allow to drip into a vessel, without pressing. Pour the juice into a preserving kettle, measuring it first, and allowing three-quarters of a pound of sugar to each pint of juice. Boil the juice about fifteen minutes before adding the sugar, which should be heating in the oven. After the sugar is added bring to a boil, and then test on a saucer.

When it jellies fill into glasses; if not, boil a few minutes longer, testing it frequently, for as a rule quince juice jellies very quickly. This makes a beautiful clear, light jelly, with a mild, delicious flavor.

GRAPE JELLY

Partially ripe grapes make better jelly than the ripe grapes. To every six pounds of grapes add three pounds of Siberian crab-apples, or apples, quartered. Stew all together until tender. Fill into a jelly bag and let drip into vessel. Measure the juice and to each pint of juice add one pound of sugar. Boil about thirty minutes before adding the sugar, then boil up after the sugar has been added. This should be ready to take off the fire in a few minutes, if the sugar has been heated in the oven before adding, but one should test it, and if it does not jelly, allow it to boil longer.

One-third of elderberry juice or one-third of rhubarb juice added to grape juice makes a nice jelly, with the flavor of grape.

RHUBARB JELLY

In making jelly, rhubarb is fine combined with other fruits. Currants and rhubarb boiled together make a delicious jelly. If black currants are used mix half and half; if red currants are used take one part currants and two of rhubarb. Use a pound of sugar to each pint of juice. Make as you would any other jelly. Rhubarb juice and peach juice are good combined in jelly, and will jelly much nicer than either used alone. Use half and half of each and three-fourths of a cup of sugar to each pint of juice. Red raspberries and rhubarb are also nice combined in jelly. Use one part of rhubarb to two of raspberries, and a pound of sugar to each pint of juice.

ELDERBERRY JELLY

Elderberries make excellent jelly when combined with Siberian crabs or with green grapes, or a little rhubarb or lemon juice. When used for jelly, elderberries should be red and not black. Blueberries should also be used for jelly before entirely ripe. If ripe, add about one-third rhubarb or green-grape juice to add to its flavor, and make it jelly nicely. Lemon juice may also be used.

PEACH-PINEAPPLE JELLY

Use equal quantities of peach and pineapple juice, and to each pint of juice add the juice of one lemon and one pound of sugar. Boil to the consistency of jelly, and fill glasses or jars.

CURRANT JELLY

In choosing currants for jelly select those that are barely ripe. Pick out leaves and poor fruit, and wash and drain. It will not be necessary to stem them. Just add enough water to prevent them from burning, and heat slowly. Mash the berries, but do not let them come to a boil. Pour into jelly bag, and allow juice to drain or drip into a vessel, without squeezing, if you wish a clear red jelly. Use granulated sugar, a pound to each pint of juice. Place the juice in a preserving kettle, and when it comes to a boil add the sugar that has been heated in the oven.

This jelly will be ready to pour into the glasses five or six minutes after the sugar is added, if none or little water has been added; but it should be tested before removing from the fire. Currant juice, combined with red raspberry, rhubarb, gooseberry, and other fruit juices, will give you a variety.

Gooseberries used for jelly should be green, and will require about a fourth cup more sugar to each pint of juice than the currants. Prepare the gooseberries as you would currants.

Red Raspberry and Currant Jelly

The raspberry is a delicious as well as wholesome fruit, and is valuable for preserving. Red raspberries make fine jelly, and are especially nice combined with currants in jelly and preserves. When combining for canning, use half and half of each kind of fruit. In making jelly, use one-third currant juice and two-thirds red raspberry juice. In making raspberry jam, you may use two-thirds red raspberries and one-third currants. In making the above jam, use three-fourths of a pound of sugar to one pound of fruit, and in making the jelly, use one pound of sugar to each pound of fruit.

BLACKBERRY JELLY AND JAM

Blackberries make a delicious jam by themselves, and are good combined with rhubarb, using three parts of the berries and two parts rhubarb. Blackberry jelly is much improved by adding a little rhubarb juice, not more than one part of rhubarb juice to two or three parts of blackberries. In making blackberry jam, press nice, ripe berries through a sieve, and then measure the pulp, and to each pint of pulp add one pound of sugar unless the berries are the very sweet ones—then do not use so much sugar.

WATERMELON JAM

A pretty pink-colored jam is made with the pink part of watermelons. Cut the pink part of watermelon up into cubes, and place in a preserv-

ing kettle with white sugar, using three pounds of
sugar to each six pounds of the fruit, and the juice
of two oranges or lemons. Stir frequently to prevent burning, and boil to the consistency of jam,
and fill into glasses, and seal. Since watermelons
contain so much water, one will have to use a good
quantity of fruit to make a small quantity of jam ;
but after trying it once you will always want a
few glasses of watermelon jam on your preserve
shelves.

GOOSEBERRY-HUCKLEBERRY JAM

To each three quarts of gooseberries add one
quart of huckleberries and four pounds of sugar.
Boil the berries together until tender, then add the
sugar. Boil to the right consistency for jam, and
fill into jars, and seal. Gooseberries and red raspberries also make an excellent combination in
jam.

RHUBARB JAM

Raspberries, blackberries, strawberries, currants,
peaches, pears, apples—all make delicious jams

when combined with rhubarb. In making strawberry-rhubarb jam take one part rhubarb and two parts strawberry. Use only the tender ends of the rhubarb. Use a pound of sugar to each pound of fruit. Place the strawberries on platters and cover with the sugar, and let the fruit stand overnight. In the morning pour off the juice into a preserving kettle, and add the rhubarb, and let boil until it begins to get thick, then add the strawberries, and cook until they are heated through. Pour into jars or glasses and seal.

This makes a pretty jam, as well as a delicious one. Red raspberry jam can be made in the same way. In making blackberry-rhubarb jam use about equal parts of each kind of fruit. A delicious preserve may be made with equal parts of pineapple and rhubarb, using a pound of sugar to each pound of fruit.

CRAB-APPLE AND GRAPE JAM

Cut half a peck of well-washed crab-apples into halves. Use the deep red ones. Place them in a kettle with three cups of water, and stew slowly until the fruit is soft, then pass through a sieve. Stew the same amount of red grapes until soft, and pass these through a sieve. Combine the pulps of the fruits. Allow one pound of sugar to each pint of pulp. Cook to the required consistency, stirring constantly. This will make a delicious red jam of fine flavor.

V

The Making of Marmalades

CHAPTER V

THE MAKING OF MARMALADES

MARMALADES differ from preserves in that the fruit is usually passed through a sieve or colander, or else mashed to a pulp with a wooden spoon, instead of being left as whole as possible. In making marmalades the fruit is cooked longer than in the making of preserves. As in the making of preserves many delicious marmalades may be made with combined fruits. We give here a variety which will likely suggest others equally as good.

ORANGE MARMALADE, No. 1

Orange marmalade is one of the universal favorites. To make a plain orange marmalade to each dozen medium sized oranges use three pounds of sugar and two lemons. Wash the oranges and lemons thoroughly. Pare off the

77

yellow rind very thinly and cut up into tiny bits. Place these in a pint of boiling water and simmer until tender. Remove all the white pith and seeds from the oranges, and cut up the pulp into bits. Add this pulp to the orange and lemon chips, the sugar and enough water to cover. Bring to a boil and simmer very slowly for about one-half hour. Rub through a colander, and return the pulp to the fire. Boil to the consistency of marmalade, pour into jars, and seal.

ORANGE MARMALADE, No. 2

To each dozen of sweet oranges take one-half dozen lemons, and one cupful and a half of English walnut meats. To each cupful of the pulp use one cupful of sugar. Place the juice of the fruits, a cupful of water, and the sugar together in a preserving kettle. Boil to the consistency of honey, then add the fruit pulp cut into small bits and the grated rind of three of the oranges and one of the lemons, and the nut meats chopped very fine. Boil to the consistency of marmalade, which is always thick, and pour into glasses.

ORANGE MARMALADE, No. 3

To each dozen of oranges use one pound of good figs, and about five pounds of sugar. Peel and shred the oranges, add the juice and grated rind of one lemon, and the grated rind of two of the oranges. Chop the figs up into bits, add water and stew until soft and tender and then add the orange pulp and sugar and boil for about twenty minutes. Pass through a coarse sieve or colander. Boil to the consistency of thick marmalade. Pour into jars and seal. One cupful of finely chopped walnut meats may be added. These orange marmalades are fine for sandwiches.

ORANGE-GRAPEFRUIT MARMALADE

To each one dozen oranges use six grapefruits, three lemons, and six tart apples. Peel, core or seed the fruits and shred them all as fine as possible. To each pint of the fruit pulp add a pint of water. Let stand in this overnight, then place over the fire and stew until tender. Add a pound of sugar to each pint of the fruit pulp, and simmer slowly until a thick marmalade, stirring frequently. Pour into glasses or jars and seal.

ORANGE-QUINCE MARMALADE

To each four pounds of quinces use a dozen oranges. Wash the quinces, core, but do not peel. Boil the quinces in three or four pints of water until tender. Crush the fruit, and drain off the juice into a vessel. Add to the quince juice the rind of a few of the oranges, using only the yellow outside rind, and none of the white pith. Simmer for fifteen minutes, then add the quince pulp passed through a sieve, and the orange pulp shredded very fine. Boil to the consistency of thick marmalade.

RHUBARB MARMALADE

To each three pounds of rhubarb use three pounds of sugar, and the juice and chopped pulp

of three oranges, and the grated peel of one.
Cut the rhubarb into about inch lengths. Cook
until soft, then mash to a pulp and add a cupful
of figs and a cupful of nut meats that have been
passed through the food chopper. Simmer slowly
until the right consistency for marmalade, and
pour into glasses or jars.

RHUBARB-PRUNE MARMALADE

Take one pound of good prunes, wash thoroughly and soak overnight in enough water to
about cover them. Simmer until tender, and
pass through a sieve ; then add a quart of rhubarb
cut up into bits, and three pounds of sugar. Boil
to a marmalade, then pour into glasses or jars and
seal.

RHUBARB-RAISIN MARMALADE

Thoroughly wash a pound of seeded raisins.
Simmer slowly in a little water until tender ; then
add one quart of rhubarb cut into small bits, and
the grated peel of one lemon or orange, and three
pounds of sugar. The raisins should be passed

through a sieve before the rhubarb is added. Simmer to the consistency of marmalade.

Pineapple-Rhubarb Marmalade

Peel and grate as many pineapples as you desire to put up in this way, and to each cupful of the grated pineapple add a cupful of rhubarb cut up into bits. Allow one pound of sugar to each pint of fruit. Mix well and stand in a cool place overnight. Cook until soft enough to pass through a sieve. Return to the preserving kettle and boil to a thick marmalade. Pour the marmalade into jars and seal.

Pineapple-Grapefruit Marmalade

To each large pineapple use three large grapefruits. Peel and grate or chop the pineapple. Cut the grapefruits into quarters, and remove the fibers and the seeds from the centers; then cut up the pulp into very small pieces, and add some orange rind, being careful not to get any of the bitter pith. If you use orange the rind of one orange will be enough, or this may be omitted. To each cupful of fruit add a cupful of sugar, and a half cupful of water. Simmer slowly to the consistency of marmalade. Pour into glasses or jars and seal while hot.

PINEAPPLE-CHERRY MARMALADE

Peel and grate the pineapple, and to each cupful of the grated pineapple add one cupful of cherry pulp. The cherries should be soaked and seeded, and then passed through a food chopper. Mix the fruits well together, then add to each pint of the pulp one pound of sugar. Simmer slowly until tender, pass through a coarse sieve, and return to the kettle, and boil to the consistency of marmalade.

PINEAPPLE-STRAWBERRY MARMALADE

Wash the strawberries quickly, stem them, and place them in a preserving kettle. Crush them, then add to each pint of the pulp one cupful of grated pineapple. To each pint of the fruit mixture add one pound of granulated sugar. Simmer slowly for twenty minutes or until a thick marmalade, and pour into jars.

PINEAPPLE-PRUNE MARMALADE

Stew the prunes until tender, after they have been soaked overnight, then pass through a sieve. Crack some of the stones, pound the kernels to a paste and add to the prune pulp. To each pint of the pulp add one cupful of grated pineapple, and one pound of sugar, and one cupful of water. Simmer slowly until a thick marmalade and pour into glasses or jars.

APPLE MARMALADE

To each three pounds of tart apples pared, cored, and quartered, add one cupful of water, an ounce of ginger root, and the juice and grated rinds of two lemons. Stew until tender, then pass through a coarse sieve. Add four pounds of sugar to this amount, and if preferred a few finely chopped almonds may be added, or English walnut meats. Boil to the consistency of marmalade, and pour into glasses or jars.

PEACH MARMALADE

Peel and seed the peaches, and stew in a little water until tender. To each pint of this peach pulp add three-fourths of a pound of sugar, and about a fourth of a cupful of water. Boil down to a thick marmalade, stirring constantly to prevent burning.

PRUNE MARMALADE

Select, wash and soak overnight three pounds of fine large prunes. Stew slowly until tender, then pass through a food chopper or a sieve. To each pint of the pulp add a cupful of stewed cranberries, and a pound of sugar. Cook to a marmalade, stirring enough to prevent sticking, and to make the marmalade smooth.

GRAPE-PEAR MARMALADE

In making this marmalade use equal parts of pears and grapes. Stew the grapes until soft,

then pass through a coarse sieve. Add to this
grape pulp an equal quantity of stewed pear pulp.
Add three-fourths of a pound of sugar to each pint
of pulp. Cook until the right consistency for marmalade, and fill jars.

WILD PLUM AND APPLE MARMALADE

Boil the plums and press through a sieve, pare
the apples, slice very thin, add to the plum pulp
and boil, stirring constantly, until the apples are
soft; then add the sugar in the proportions of one
pound of sugar to each pint of pulp if tart apples
are used; and from two-thirds to one-half, if sweet
apples are used. Cook until fine and thick, and
then fill glasses or jars and seal.

CURRANT-CHERRY MARMALADE

For this marmalade use the red cherries and red
currants. Add just enough water to prevent
burning, and simmer slowly until tender; then
pass through a coarse sieve or colander. Place in
a preserving kettle, and add to each pint of pulp

one pound of sugar. Boil slowly to the consistency of marmalade; then fill glasses or jars and seal.

PEAR MARMALADE

Choose nice, fine-flavored pears. Pare, and cut up into bits, and drop into cold water. When ready to use drain, weigh, and to each six pounds of the fruit add one lemon sliced very thin. Pour over just enough water to cover, and simmer slowly until tender. Pass the fruit through a coarse sieve; then add the sugar, using three-fourths of a pound of sugar to each pint of pulp. Heat the sugar in the oven before adding it. Cook slowly, stirring almost constantly until it forms a thick marmalade. Pour into jars or glasses.

PLUM AND CRAB-APPLE MARMALADE

Wash nice large red Siberian crab-apples, cut out the stems, blossoms and all black specks and knots; add a small amount of water and steam or simmer slowly until the pulp is soft enough to press through a rather coarse sieve. Allow one-third as many plums as apples. Red plums are the nicest for this purpose, although damson plums may be used. Stew or steam the plums until tender. Pass through a sieve, and add to the crab-apple pulp.

· Allow one pound of sugar to each pound or pint of pulp. Heat the sugar in the oven and add to the pulp after it has come to a boil. Cook slowly and steadily, stirring almost constantly until it is a thick jam.

Put into jars or glasses.

QUINCE MARMALADE

Take nice ripe quinces, pare, quarter and core. To add one-third apples will make this marmalade not so strong, and improve it for many. Place in a baking dish and add a little sweet cider, just enough to about half cover the fruit. Cover and bake very slowly in the oven until the fruit is very tender, adding more cider or water as it is absorbed. When done or tender add three-fourths of a cup of sugar to each cup of baked quince. Cook until it becomes a jelly-like mass, stirring constantly to prevent burning, then turn into glasses. Water may be used instead of the sweet cider if preferred, but the flavor of the cider blends perfectly with the quinces.

Tomato Marmalade

The small yellow tomatoes are nice for this purpose. Peel and measure, and to each pound of fruit add a pound of sugar. To each seven pounds of the fruit use the juice of a half dozen oranges, and the juice of three lemons. Use the grated rind of three of the oranges and one of the lemon, using only the yellow part, as the white pith is bitter. Boil to the consistency of marmalade, stirring constantly. Fill preserve jars and seal.

VI

Spiced and Pickled Fruits

CHAPTER VI

SPICED AND PICKLED FRUITS

FRUITS, such as peaches, pears, plums and such like, are the most satisfactory for pickling purposes, but berries are also fine spiced. Spiced and pickled fruits make nice relishes to be eaten with meats, and the larger fruits are nice to include in the children's school lunches.

None but ripe, firm fruits should be chosen for pickling, and only the best cider vinegar. This may be weakened to suit the taste.

GINGERED PEARS

Hard pears may be used for this purpose. Pare, core and cut into fine shavings. Weigh and to each pound of fruit allow one pound of sugar, one ounce of green ginger root, and the juice of half of a lemon. Save the rind. Place the pear chips in a porcelain-lined kettle, and add the sugar and lemon juice, and let stand overnight or for several hours at least. Simmer the ginger root and the lemon rind in the sugar and vinegar for about thirty minutes. Cook the pear chips in this until transparent, and there is a thick syrup formed around them.

Fill glass jars, and seal while hot.

SPICED STRAWBERRIES

Strawberries retain their color better when spiced than when canned, since the vinegar helps to retain the red color. To each cupful of vinegar used add two cupfuls of sugar. Spices may be used or not as liked. Many persons prefer the flavor obtained by adding a little stick cinnamon or a few cloves and bits of mace. Boil the vinegar and sugar to a thick syrup and then add firm berries and simmer until transparent. Place the berries in jars with a strainer, and boil the syrup down until a little thicker and pour over the berries to overflowing. Seal at once.

CHERRY PICKLES

To each five pounds of cherries use one pint of vinegar, three pounds of sugar, and one teaspoonful each of ground cinnamon and mace, and a few cloves. Tie the spices up in a cheese-cloth bag, and allow them to simmer with the sugar and vinegar for about fifteen minutes. Add the fruit and simmer slowly for about twenty minutes. Fill into jars and seal while hot. Cherries may be stemmed and stoned for these pickles, or the stems and stones may be retained if desired.

PINEAPPLE PICKLE

Pineapple pickles are not so common as some others, and have a piquancy all their own. To make them slice ripe pineapples, and then skin and remove core with a sharp knife or corer. Cut into quarters or eighths, or the rounds may be left as they are. To each seven pounds of the fruit use three and a half pounds of granulated sugar, a tablespoonful each of cinnamon and mace, and one teaspoonful each of allspice and cloves, and if preferred a bit of ginger root. Tie the spices up in a bag, and add to the vinegar. To each pint of strong vinegar add one cupful of water, and the sugar.

Boil to the consistency of honey, and then add the pineapple and simmer several minutes. Take off the fire and let stand twelve hours. Drain off the syrup, and boil several minutes, then pour over the pineapple arranged in jars, and seal while hot.

Spiced Peach Pickles

Either free-stone or clings may be used for this purpose. Peel, and leave whole. To each seven pounds of fruit use four pounds of sugar, and one ounce each of cinnamon and allspice, and one teaspoonful each of cloves and mace, one pint of vinegar and one pint of water. Place the sugar, water and spices tied in a muslin bag together in a preserving kettle, and bring to a boil; then drop in the peaches and cook until heated through. Let stand in this syrup overnight; then pour off

into a kettle, and add the vinegar. Boil down
to the consistency of honey, pour over the peaches,
arranged in glass jars, and seal.

Stuffed Spiced Peaches

To make these use large, firm free-stone peaches,
peel and halve.   In the center of each half place
a bit of ginger root.   Place the two halves together, and keep in place with splints from stick
cinnamon.   Proceed as in the above recipe only
omitting the spices.   The ginger root and cinnamon give the desired spiciness to these pickles.
Use white vinegar or clear vinegar, and white
sugar for these pickles.

Spiced Quinces and Apples

Peel the sweet apples and quinces, halve and
core.   Simmer slowly in a little water until nearly
tender ; then remove and place in a spiced syrup
made by adding sugar, water, and spices.   Use
four pounds of sugar to each seven pounds of fruit,

one ounce each of ginger root, cinnamon, cloves and allspice. Tie the spices in a muslin bag. Remove the quinces and apples from syrup, and fill into glass jars. Boil the syrup down a little more, pour over the fruit, and seal.

SPICED SWEET APPLES

Peel and quarter nice large sweet apples. To each seven pounds of the fruit add four pounds of sugar, one quart of vinegar, one pint of water, and one ounce each of allspice and cinnamon tied up in a muslin bag. In each quarter of apple stick one or two cloves, and add to the syrup, and boil until tender. Remove and fill into jars and boil the syrup down until thick, and pour over the apples. If you wish a dark pickle use brown sugar, and if you wish them clear and transparent use white sugar and clear vinegar. Simmer the fruit in a syrup spiced only with stick cinnamon and a little ginger root or lemon rind, and add the vinegar after the fruit has been removed to jars.

MINTED SWEET APPLES

Follow the above recipe only instead of spices add a cupful of mint tea made by simmering one cupful of fresh green mint in a pint of water or a half cupful of dried mint. Strain before adding. Use one cupful of water instead of the pint.

PICKLED FIGS

To seven pounds of ripe figs allow three pounds of sugar, one pint of vinegar, one pint of water, and one ounce each of cloves, allspice, mace and cinnamon tied up in a muslin bag. Boil the figs in the syrup until tender and fill into jars. Boil the spiced syrup down until it has the consistency of honey, pour over the figs, and seal.

QUINCE SWEET PICKLES

For these pickles use only the choicest, ripe yellow quinces of fine flavor. These quinces may be pared or left unpared as liked. If not pared be sure to remove all down and specks. Cut in slices about an inch thick, and weigh. Steam until tender. Make a syrup, using for each four pounds of fruit two pounds of sugar, a cupful of vinegar of medium strength, and a cupful of water, a teaspoonful each of allspice, cloves, and a half ounce of stick cinnamon. Tie the spices in a bag of cheese-cloth, boil with the sugar and vinegar for five minutes, skim well, and pour boiling hot over the fruit. Let this stand overnight, then drain off the syrup, and boil down. Add the quinces and heat through, then put into jars, and pour the syrup, which should be the consistency of molasses, over the fruit.

Seal while hot.

WATERMELON SWEET PICKLE

Cut up the watermelon into strips, and remove all the green rind and soft inner pulp. Cut into cubes and soak in weak brine overnight, allowing about one-half cupful of salt to a gallon of water. To each seven pounds of fruit use four pounds of granulated sugar, one pint of vinegar, one pint of water, several sticks of cinnamon, a bit of ginger

root or lemon rind or both if desired.   Place the
sugar, water, and spices together in a kettle, and
add the melon, and simmer until tender.   Remove from the fire, and let stand several hours in
the syrup.   Put syrup over fire again and add the
vinegar, and boil to a thick syrup, and pour over
the melon in glass jars.   Seal.

CANTELOUPE SWEET PICKLE

Cut the canteloupe into sections, peel, and
remove the green rind and the soft inner part.
Soak in a weak brine overnight.   Proceed as in
making the watermelon pickle, only add instead
of the ginger root a teaspoonful of mace and a
few cloves tied up in a muslin bag.

SPICED GOOSEBERRIES

Use the ripe gooseberries for spicing.   To each
seven pounds of fruit use four pounds of sugar,
one tablespoonful of cinnamon (or two or three
sticks of cinnamon broken into bits), one tablespoonful of whole cloves, one tablespoonful of

allspice, four blades of mace, and, if liked, a bit of ginger root or orange rind.   Place the spices in a muslin bag.   Make a thick syrup of the sugar and enough water to dissolve, add the fruit and the vinegar, using about a pint to the above amount of fruit.   Remove the fruit with a skimmer and fill into jars.   Boil the spiced syrup down to a thick syrup, pour over the fruit, and seal.

SPICED BLUEBERRIES

Blueberries are good spiced.   To each quart of fruit allow about three-fourths of a pound of sugar, one-half cupful of vinegar, a teaspoonful each of cinnamon and allspice.   Tie the spices in thin muslin bags and boil with the sugar and vinegar, and one-half cupful of water, add the berries, heat slowly and boil for about five minutes.

SPICED PLUMS

Prepare a syrup, allowing one pound of sugar to one of plums, and to each three pounds of sugar one pint of pure cider vinegar.   Simmer

twenty minutes.   Allow four tablespoonfuls each
of whole spices, cinnamon, broken in pieces,
cloves and allspice, one tablespoonful of blades of
mace, to peck of ripe plums.   Prick the plums.
Add the spices to the syrup, and pour over fruit
boiling hot.   Let stand in stone jar three days,
then drain plums from syrup.   Put into quart
fruit jars.   Place syrup in porcelain-lined kettle
and boil down until quite thick, and pour over
fruit until jars are full.   Place covers on jars and
seal.   Let stand until cold, then try tops to see if
air-tight.   Put away in a cool, dry place.

SWEET PEAR PICKLE

Small pears should be pickled whole, while the
large ones should be halved and cored, and all
should be peeled.   Use to each five pounds of
pears two pounds of sugar, one quart of water,
one pint of good vinegar, one teaspoonful each of
cloves, cinnamon and allspice, and one tablespoonful of ginger root.   If you wish these a little
stronger with vinegar, use one quart of vinegar

and one pint of water. When the syrup has come to the boiling point, put the fruit in and simmer slowly until tender, then fill carefully into jars, pour the hot syrup over them, and seal.

PICKLED MUSKMELONS

Take ripe muskmelons, cut off the rind and remove the seeds, and cut into uniform pieces. For every five pounds of melon use one quart of vinegar, one pint of water, three pounds of sugar, one tablespoonful each of cloves and cinnamon, and one-half teaspoonful of allspice and mace. Tie the spices in a bag and boil in the vinegar. Place the fruit in the syrup when it has come to a boil, and boil until clear and tender. Remove from the syrup with a strainer or silver fork and place in jars. Boil the syrup a few minutes longer, pour over the pickles, and seal.

PICKLED GRAPES

Choose nice large grapes that are not too ripe. Wash and cut off by the stem, and place in a jar.

Make a syrup of vinegar, sugar and spices, as for the other pickled fruit, and when boiling pour over the grapes in the jars and let stand until cool, then pour back in the kettle—you should have a little more syrup than will fill the jars in the first place, to allow for boiling away—and boil down until the syrup begins to thicken a little, then pour over the grapes again, to overflowing, and seal while hot.

Spiced Siberian Crabs and Plums

Use the nice red-cheeked Siberian crabs for this purpose, and the large red plums. Pick over carefully, but do not peel. Prick the skins. Steam the apples and plums until tender, but keep them as whole as possible. For each four pounds allow four pounds of sugar, one pint of vinegar, and a teaspoonful each of cinnamon and allspice. If preferred one or two cloves can be stuck into each apple and plum. Simmer slowly until clear. This is excellent when served with meats.

Spiced Currants

Place six pounds of stemmed currants in alternate layers with four pounds of sugar in a preserving kettle, and let stand several hours. Turn off the juice and boil until it jellies; then add the currants, one tablespoonful of cinnamon, one teaspoonful each of allspice and cloves, and one cupful of vinegar. Boil to a thick sauce, and fill into jars. This is particularly good to serve with meats.

VII

Pickled Vegetables

CHAPTER VII

PICKLED VEGETABLES

CORN AND CABBAGE PICKLE

To each large head of cabbage use one dozen ears of sweet corn. Cook the two vegetables separately in slightly salted water until tender. Chop the cabbage, and cut the corn from the cob and combine the two. Make a spiced vinegar as you did for the other pickles, and pour over. Simmer slowly in this for fifteen or twenty minutes; then fill jars and seal.

SUCCOTASH PICKLES

To each quart of golden-wax pod beans use one dozen ears of corn. Boil the two vegetables separately in salted water. Cut the corn from the cob, and cut the beans up into about half inch lengths. Cover with a spiced vinegar, and simmer together a short time before filling into the jars.

Ripe Cucumber Sweet Pickles

Choose good, firm, nearly ripe cucumbers, pare and core, cut into thick slices. Soak in salted water overnight; then in the morning drain off. Place in a preserving kettle one quart of vinegar, one cupful of water, two pounds of sugar, and two tablespoonfuls of mixed spice tied up in a bag. Use this amount for about a half gallon of the sliced cucumbers. Boil the sugar, water and spices to a syrup, then add the cucumbers and cook until the cucumbers are tender. Fill jars, and seal while hot.

Pickled Sweet Red Peppers

Choose large red sweet peppers, and after washing well remove the seeds and pulp. Cut them in rounds, and place in a kettle or jar and pour boiling water over them to which has been added a half cupful of salt to a half gallon of water. Let stand in this brine for several hours, then drain off in a colander. Pour some water over them, or let soak a few moments in cold water. Place in a preserving kettle one quart of vinegar, one pint of water, two pounds of light brown sugar, and a little bag of mixed spices. This amount will be about right for a gallon of peppers. Place the peppers in this, and let boil until tender. Remove with a skimmer and place in jars. Boil the spiced vinegar to a syrup, pour over the pickles to overflowing, and seal.

PICKLED STUFFED RED PEPPERS

Cut the stem end from large red peppers, remove the seed and soak in a weak brine overnight. In the morning drain off the brine. For the filling use cooked red beets, raw red cabbage, and ripe tomatoes. To this mixture a few tiny red peppercorns may be added. Fill this chopped mixture solidly into the empty peppers. Fasten on the removed tops of the peppers with splints of cinnamon, and place in jars. Make a spiced vinegar as for other vegetable pickles and when scalding hot pour over, and allow to stand twenty-four hours, then drain off and boil up the syrup again, and pour over the peppers again. Repeat once more. The last time seal while hot.

PICKLED BEETS

For pickling use young, tender beets. Wash them well, cook and peel, as usual. If small, they should be left whole; if large, slice in thick slices. To make the pickling syrup, add to one pint of vinegar one cup of water, and four pounds of sugar, to each seven or eight pounds of the beets. Boil in this one dozen or more cloves and two sticks of cinnamon. Skim off all scum that may arise, then add the beets and cook about ten minutes. Remove with a strainer or fork and fill carefully into glass jars—the wide-mouthed jars are the best for most pickles. Pour the syrup over the beets in the can until overflowing, and seal while hot.

PICKLED BEANS IN POD

The large golden-wax or white pod beans are the finest for pickling. Cook these in slightly salted water until tender, but be careful not to cook them too long, or they will get soft. Drain and fill into jars. Boil together two cups of vinegar, one cup of water, two cups of sugar, and a little bag of mixed spice. Pour over the cooked beans in the jars and seal tight. Use about one heaping teaspoonful of salt for each quart of water in which the beans are boiled.

PICKLED ONIONS

Choose the small silver-skinned variety. Peel and place overnight in a brine that will float an egg. In the morning drain. Put over the fire to boil enough vinegar to cover the onions and about one teaspoonful each of allspice and cloves to each quart of onions. Fill the onions into the jars, adding a few small red peppers, then pour over them the scalding hot vinegar and seal. A tablespoonful of sugar added to each quart of onions will improve these for many. If preferred, cook the onions until tender before placing them in the jars. Either way will make good pickles.

GREEN TOMATO PICKLE

Slice without peeling one gallon of green tomatoes, and peel and slice one quart of onions. Arrange in layers in a crock, placing salt between each layer, using about one cup of salt for this amount of tomatoes. Pour over one quart of water and let stand until morning, then drain off the water in the morning. Place in a saucepan or kettle one quart of vinegar, one cupful of water, two cupfuls of sugar, one teaspoonful each of ground mustard and pepper, one-half teaspoonful each of allspice and cloves—or one tablespoonful of mixed spice may be used,—the spices tied up in a little bag and boiled in the vinegar. Place the tomatoes in this and boil until tender, then fill jars.

SWEET CUCUMBER PICKLES

Take one-half peck small cucumbers—they should be about two inches long and as uniform in size as possible. Pour over enough brine to cover them, using about one cupful of salt to one gallon of water. Let stand overnight. In the morning place in a kettle three pints of vinegar, one pint of water, one and a half pounds of granulated sugar, one-fourth cupful of cinnamon, broken into pieces, one tablespoonful of cloves, a few tiny red peppers, and one teaspoonful of mace—or, if preferred, mixed spice may be used—but whatever kind is used, tie up in little cheese-cloth bags.

· Drain the cucumbers, and wash in two or three waters to freshen them up some, then place them in the vinegar mixture, after it has boiled long enough to get the spices extracted—about twenty minutes. Bring just to the boil again, after the cucumbers have been put in, and then take out the cucumbers with a skimmer and pack them into jars.

Boil the vinegar up again and pour over the pickles in the jars and seal.

WHITE MIXED PICKLES

Take one quart of small white onions, one quart of peeled and sliced cucumbers, using them when large and white-fleshed, one quart of white chopped cabbage, one pint of white celery cut into inch lengths, and about one-half cupful of horseradish. Soak these vegetables separately in weak brine overnight, then in the morning drain and cook in half water and half vinegar, until tender, keeping each vegetable separate. Boil one quart of white beans in slightly salted water. Place in a kettle one quart of vinegar, one pint of water, one pound of white sugar, one teaspoonful of white mustard, one-half teaspoonful of white pepper, and one tablespoonful of celery seed. Place the vegetables in this, bring just to the boil, fill jars and seal.

GREEN MIXED PICKLES

Take two quarts of small, whole cucumbers, two quarts of green tomatoes, sliced, one quart of green beans, one quart of green peppers, and two quarts of green leaves of cabbage. Soak the vegetables in salt water overnight. Boil in half water and half vinegar in the morning, first draining off

the brine. Make a spiced vinegar, using enough
vinegar and in the same proportion the other ingredients as they are mentioned in the white
pickle recipe. Green radish pods or nasturtiums
may be added, instead of the horseradish. Line
a kettle with horseradish leaves and place in the
vegetables, pour over the hot vinegar mixture and
bring to a boil. Lift out the vegetables with a
skimmer and fill into jars until overflowing, and
seal.

RED MIXED PICKLE

To make this red pickle use one quart of red
chopped cabbage, one quart of sweet red peppers,
one quart of chopped red beets, and one quart of
red kidney beans, shelled from the pods before
being quite ripe. Put all the vegetables in salt
water overnight, except the beans. Boil separately in the morning, first draining off the brine,
then proceed as in making the other pickles.
Spices as suggested above under "Sweet Cucumber Pickles" may be used with a few tiny

red peppers, or you may use only a little bag of mixed spices.

MIXED SWEET PICKLES

Cook all the vegetables separately and keep them as whole as possible. The vegetables required are: two dozen small cucumbers, one quart silver-skinned onions, one quart of green tomatoes cut into cubes, one quart of tender, golden-wax stringless beans, one quart of shelled lima beans —not ripe but old enough to shell nicely—one quart of carrots cut into half-inch slices, two heads of celery cut into bits, and two heads of cauliflower. Cover the vegetables with a weak brine, and let stand overnight, keeping each kind of vegetable separate. In the morning, cook in the water in which they have been soaked, until tender, then drain.

Let a gallon of vinegar come to a boil, add two pounds of sugar, a bag of mixed spices, about four or five ounces, and four teaspoonfuls of celery salt. Let remain over the fire until the

spices have become well blended with the vine.
gar. Arrange the different vegetables in glass
jars the way they will look best, then pour over
them the boiling hot vinegar, filling the jars to
overflowing, then seal. If you do not have
enough vinegar to cover all the vegetables, prepare a little more; and also add a little more
salt if needed.

PICKLED CARROTS

Pickled carrots are something new, and many
people like them prepared in this way who do
not relish the fresh vegetable. To make, choose
an equal number of deep yellow and light yellow
carrots; peel and cut into strips. Boil in slightly
salted water until tender. Drain, then cover with
spiced vinegar, using a quart of vinegar and one
cupful of water to a gallon of carrots. Add to
the vinegar and water one pound of sugar, two
ounces of mixed spices tied in a thin muslin bag,
and bring to a boil. Then add the carrots, and boil
a few minutes longer, after which put them in jars.

Ripe Tomato Pickle

Take two dozen medium-sized firm red tomatoes, one quart of red cabbage, six small peppercorns, two ounces of mixed spices, one quart of chopped beets, one quart of chopped red peppers, one pound of sugar, and one quart of vinegar.

Boil the cabbage and chopped peppers in slightly salted water for about fifteen minutes and drain. Boil the beets in their skins, and when cold remove skins and chop.

Place the vinegar, sugar, and spices (tied in a muslin bag) in a preserving kettle; when the mixture begins to boil add the tomatoes, peeled and sliced, and the other vegetables. Heat thoroughly; put into jars. Boil the vinegar and spices several minutes longer and pour over the vegetables. This makes an excellent red pickle. Salt should be added to make it savory.

Green Tomato Sweet Pickle

To each seven pounds of tomatoes use about one-half dozen medium-sized onions, sliced, three

pounds of sugar, one pint of strong vinegar, and
one pint of water, an ounce of cinnamon, and one-
half ounce each of cloves and allspice—or, better,
two ounces of mixed spices. Cover the tomatoes
with a brine, using about one cupful of salt to a
gallon of water. In the morning drain off well.
Place the vinegar, sugar, spices (tied in a muslin
bag), and the tomatoes in a preserving kettle and
simmer slowly until tender. Put into jars and
seal. If mixed spices are not used add a teaspoonful of whole pepper.

PICCALILLI

Take one peck of green tomatoes, one dozen of
small onions, one quart of vinegar, one pint of
water, a horseradish root, one head of cabbage,
one-half dozen of cucumbers, two pounds of brown
sugar, and mixed spices.

Slice and chop the tomatoes, also the cabbage,
the onions, and the cucumbers. Soak in a weak
brine overnight, and in the morning drain off
well. Place the vinegar, water, sugar, mixed

spices (tied in a muslin bag), and the root of horseradish in the preserving kettle; add the vegetables and cook slowly until tender. If not salty enough, add salt to taste. Put into jars and seal.

TOMATO MANGOES

Select for these mangoes fully matured green tomatoes. Cut a slice off the stem end and remove the seeds and part of the pulp, leaving good-sized cavities in each tomato. Fill these cavities with chopped cabbage, onions, celery and a little horseradish, pack in as solidly as possible, and then fasten on the slice that has been removed; this can either be tied on with strings, or kept in place by means of splints cut from stick cinnamon. Cover these stuffed tomatoes with a strong brine, and let them stand in it overnight, then drain off. Parboil in water to which has been added a pint of vinegar. Remove and drain.

To each seven pounds of the tomatoes use four pounds of sugar, one quart of vinegar, one pint of water, and two ounces of mixed spices. Pack the mangoes in stone jars, and pour the boiling hot vinegar syrup over them. Allow to stand for twenty-four hours, pour off the vinegar, and boil again until about the consistency of honey; then pour it over the mangoes again. Keep tightly covered.

CAULIFLOWER PICKLES

To each six heads of cauliflower use about three pints of strong vinegar, and one pint of water, three cupfuls of light brown sugar, two ounces of mixed spices, three green peppers, or a half dozen small red peppercorns. Soak the cauliflower in brine overnight, and drain off; then in the morning boil until tender in a little water.

Place the vinegar, sugar and spices in a preserving kettle and allow to simmer for fifteen or twenty minutes; then add the cauliflower and simmer a few minutes longer. Arrange the cauliflower in jars, and pour the boiling hot vinegar over it, and seal.

CELERY PICKLE

To each two quarts of chopped celery add one quart of chopped white cabbage, and one cupful of chopped Spanish onions. Soak overnight in a salt brine—not too strong. About a half cupful of salt to a gallon of water. In the morning drain off the water.

Place the celery mixture in a preserving vessel, add enough water to cover and cook slowly until tender. Add one quart of vinegar, a cupful of sugar, an ounce of mixed spices, also one tablespoonful of celery salt. Simmer a few minutes in this and fill into jars and seal.

PICKLED NASTURTIUM SEEDS

Gather the nasturtium seeds as soon as the petals of the flowers have dropped. Make a salt brine as you would for other pickles, and soak the seeds in this for at least twenty-four hours. Drain off the brine, and soak in cold water for an hour or more. Make a good spiced vinegar, pour over seeds, and seal.

PICKLED WALNUTS

To make these pickles use green walnuts that are soft enough to prick with a needle. Let the walnuts soak two or three days in a strong brine, made by using about three cupfuls of salt to each gallon of water. Drain them and let soak in cold water until they are the right saltiness; then cover with cold vinegar and let them stand in this for several days, or weeks will be all the better. Then drain off the vinegar into a preserving kettle, and add to each half gallon of vinegar one pint of water, one cupful of brown sugar, a dozen peppercorns, a half ounce of cinnamon, cloves and mace, and two ounces of mustard seeds. Pour boiling hot over the walnuts after the spices have simmered a while in the vinegar. Let the walnuts stand in this twenty-four hours, drain off and reheat, then pour over the walnuts again.

The walnuts should be just about right for pickling in July.

MUSTARD PICKLES

To make this mustard pickle different vegetable

combinations may be used. The combination given here will be found excellent, however. Take two quarts of small cucumbers, or the same amount of sliced cucumbers if they are large, two quarts of very small white onions, one quart of cauliflower cut up into bits, one quart of celery, one quart of green tomatoes, and a quart of green and red sweet peppers mixed. Soak these vegetables in a brine overnight, using about a half cupful of salt to each two quarts of water. It is best to soak the vegetables separately. In the morning drain off the brine, and cook the vegetables until tender. The onions and cauliflower are best cooked without placing them in the brine, or they may be placed in the brine after being cooked.

Place in a preserving kettle four quarts of good vinegar, and add two pounds of light brown sugar. Let the mixture come to a boil; then stir in a paste made of one pint of water, one cupful of flour, one-half pound of mustard, one tablespoonful of tumeric, and one teaspoonful each of

cinnamon and allspice. Let this come to a boil,
stirring all the time. Add the cooked vegetables,
and bring to a scald, and fill into jars. If you
don't care to have these pickles so strong of
mustard use only one-quarter pound of mustard,
and add one-half ounce of curry powder.

Green Pepper Mangoes

Take the desired number of large green peppers
and remove the seeds. Soak them in a rather
strong brine for two or three days, then drain
off. The stem ends only should be cut off. For
the filling use chopped cabbage, chopped onion,
chopped cucumbers and chopped green tomatoes,
a bit of horseradish, celery and mustard seed, and
any spices preferred, such as mace, cloves and
allspice, and salt to taste. Pack this filling into
the peppers, place the tops on, fastening with
splints of cinnamon or with cord. Pack in a jar,
and pour spiced vinegar over, and seal. If much
spice is used in the filling do not use so much
in the vinegar.

DILL PICKLES

Good-sized cucumbers should be used for these. Pack the pickles in stone jars with dill between each layer, and a few bay leaves picked to pieces. To each quart of water allow two tablespoonfuls of salt, and one-third quart of vinegar. Boil and skim, and pour over the pickles. Cover well, and keep the pickles under the liquid by using a weight on top.

SOUR CUCUMBER PICKLES

Use small cucumbers for this purpose. To each two quarts of cucumbers use one pint of vinegar, and two tablespoonfuls of salt, and one tablespoonful of mustard, a few small peppercorns, or a bit of horseradish. Pack the pickles in jars, after they have been thoroughly washed, and pour the vinegar over them to overflowing; then seal, or if for immediate use they may be packed in crocks.

SPANISH PICKLE

For this pickle use green and ripe tomatoes, cucumbers, celery, beets, red and green peppers, and onions. Use an equal quantity of each. Cabbage may be also added. Run all these vegetables through a coarse meat chopper, after they have been allowed to stand in a strong brine overnight and then drained. Place on the stove with vinegar to cover, sugar and spices, using for each two quarts of vinegar two pounds of sugar, one ounce of mustard seed, and two ounces of mixed spices. Boil slowly until thick, fill jars, and seal.

OIL PICKLES

Oil cucumber pickles are made like other pickles, only a cupful of olive or other salad oil is added to each quart of vinegar.

VIII

Relishes for Winter Use

CHAPTER VIII

RELISHES FOR WINTER USE

Every housewife desires to put up for winter and early spring use relishes to serve with meats and other heavy dishes. Delicious relishes can be made with both fruits and vegetables, and the recipes that follow will afford you a variety of the very best.

Blackberry Relish

To each gallon of ripe blackberries allow two pounds of sugar and one cupful of vinegar, and half an ounce each of cinnamon, cloves and allspice. Place the berries, vinegar and sugar in a preserving kettle. Tie the spices together in a thin muslin or cheese-cloth bag, and add to the fruit. Boil slowly several minutes; then remove, and when cool pass the berries through a sieve, fine enough to remove the seeds. Return to fire and boil as thick as ordinary catsup. Put into jars or bottles and seal.

PLUM CATSUP

Wash and drain a gallon of damson or any kind of plums. Cover with a quart of water and cook slowly until tender; then press through a sieve, rubbing through as much pulp as possible. To this amount of plums allow two pounds of sugar, one tablespoonful of cinnamon, and one teaspoonful of allspice and cloves. Simmer, and when the consistency of catsup, put into jars or bottles.

GREEN GRAPE CATSUP

Select grapes that are just turning purple, and to each gallon of grapes add two pounds of sugar, one cupful of good cider vinegar, and one tablespoonful each of cinnamon, cloves and allspice, and one teaspoonful each of pepper and salt. Stew the grapes in just enough water to start the juice flowing; then pass through a sieve. Place the pulp, sugar, vinegar and salt together in a preserving kettle. Tie the spices up in a muslin bag and add to the fruit. Simmer slowly until of the consistency of ordinary catsup. Ripe grape catsup may be made in the same manner.

GRAPE CHUTNEY

To each two quarts of grapes add two quarts of chopped apples, and a pound of seeded and chopped raisins, one pound of sugar and one cupful of lemon juice. Put all together in a preserving kettle and add a bag containing a tablespoonful each of allspice and cloves, a half ounce of ginger and stick cinnamon. Simmer slowly, and when about the consistency of a thick pureé, season with a heaping teaspoonful of salt, and add some paprika or pepper. If preferred, vinegar may be used instead of the lemon juice, and if you wish it more tart, add a cupful of vinegar besides the lemon juice.

SPICED CURRANT RELISH

To each gallon red currants allow one and a half pounds of sugar, one pint of vinegar, one pound of seeded raisins, one tablespoonful each of cinnamon, allspice and cloves, tied up in a bag. Boil until the currants and raisins are tender, then remove with a strainer and put into jars. Boil the syrup down to a thick consistency, pour over the fruit, and seal while hot.

CUCUMBER RELISH

Use ripe cucumbers, and after removing the seeds grate down the pulp into a bowl, and to each quart of pulp add a heaping teaspoonful of salt. Let stand several hours, then drain off the liquid. To each quart of pulp allow three large white onions, one pint of clear vinegar, and one teaspoonful each of pepper, ground cloves and allspice—and if not salt enough, add a little more salt. Bring to a boil, then add to the above amount half a cup of sugar, and simmer slowly to the consistency of ordinary catsup.

CELERY RELISH

Half a dozen bunches of celery, two quarts of

green tomatoes, two quarts of ripe tomatoes, one pint of onions, three green peppers. Chop very fine. Soak in weak brine overnight, and drain in the morning. Place in an agate or porcelain-lined preserving kettle with two quarts of good cider vinegar, three cupfuls of sugar, one table-spoonful each of mustard seed and salt, one ounce of celery seed, and one teaspoonful each of cloves, allspice and cinnamon. Bring gradually to the boiling point, and simmer slowly two hours. Put into jars or bottles, and seal while hot.

Pepper Catsup

Four dozen red peppers, cut up into small pieces. To these add a half dozen small onions, chopped fine, and half a cup grated horseradish, two tablespoonfuls each of celery seed and mustard seed, one quart of vinegar, and one pint of water. Bring to a boil, and let simmer for a quarter of an hour; then add one pound of brown sugar. Boil to the consistency of ordinary catsup, and put into jars or bottles, and seal while hot.

Mixed Vegetable Relish

Two quarts of finely chopped cabbage, one dozen small onions, half a dozen chopped peppers, half a dozen cucumbers, chopped, and one quart of chopped green tomatoes. Place these ingredients over the fire with one quart of vinegar, one quart of water, one pound of brown sugar, and two tablespoonfuls of celery seed, one tablespoonful of grated horseradish, one tablespoonful of ground mustard, and one teaspoonful each of allspice, cinnamon, mace and cloves, with salt and pepper to taste. Cook slowly, stirring constantly, until thick and smooth. Put into jars and bottles and seal.

Chili Sauce

To a gallon of fine ripe tomatoes that have been peeled and cut into bits, add half a dozen medium-sized white onions, chopped very fine; half a dozen green peppers, also chopped fine. Put all together in a preserving kettle and add one quart of good cider vinegar, one pint of water, one cup of sugar, one level teaspoonful each of cayenne pepper and ground mustard, one table-spoonful each of ground celery seed and cinnamon, and a teaspoonful each of mace and cloves, and salt to taste.   Simmer slowly, stir often, and boil until a little thicker than catsup.   Put into jars or bottles and seal while hot.

APPLE CHUTNEY

To a dozen tart apples that have been peeled and cut up into bits add half a dozen large tomatoes that have been scalded, peeled and cut up, two sweet green peppers, and one cup of seeded raisins.   Place these in a preserving kettle with one quart of good cider vinegar and one pound of brown sugar, two tablespoonfuls of salt, one teaspoonful each of mustard and ginger, and half a teaspoonful of pepper.

Cook slowly for an hour, put into glass jars and seal.

GOOSEBERRY CATSUP

To seven pounds of gooseberries (either ripe or green) allow four pounds of sugar, one pint of vinegar, if the berries are ripe, or one cup, if green, one tablespoonful each of ground cloves and cinnamon, and one teaspoonful each of ginger and allspice. If you wish a little mustard or pepper may be added. Boil all together, stirring constantly, to the consistency of catsup. Seal in bottles or jars.

CURRANT CATSUP

To six pounds of washed and stemmed currants add three pounds of light-brown sugar, one pint of vinegar, one tablespoonful of cinnamon, one teaspoonful each of cloves and allspice, and half a teaspoonful of pepper. Boil to the consistency of catsup.

Pass through a sieve, boil five minutes longer, and bottle or seal in jars.

GOOSEBERRY CHUTNEY

For this chutney use gooseberries that are just beginning to ripen. Add to each pound of gooseberries a quarter of a pound of seeded, chopped raisins.   To each four pounds of this fruit mixture add half a teaspoonful of red pepper, two pounds of light-brown sugar, two tablespoonfuls of mustard seed, one tablespoonful each of salt and ginger, and about two scant quarts of vinegar.   A little chopped onion or garlic may be added. Simmer slowly about an hour, stirring frequently. Seal up in bottles or small jars.   Good to serve with meats.

TOMATO CHUTNEY

Excellent tomato chutney is made by taking a peck of green tomatoes, a half dozen onions and the same number of large green peppers.   Cut the tomatoes into thick slices, chop the onions and peppers very fine.   Mix all thoroughly together. Sprinkle salt over all, and allow to stand overnight; then drain off the salt water, and place the mixture in a porcelain-lined kettle.   Stir in the tomato mixture two quarts of good cider vinegar, two pounds of brown sugar, one-half ounce each of ground mustard, mustard seeds, cloves, allspice, cinnamon, black pepper, and one-fourth ounce of cayenne pepper. Mix this well into the tomatoes and boil all slowly for at least two hours.

Pour into cans or jars and seal.

A Good Green Relish

In making the green relish, use two quarts of chopped green tomatoes, two quarts of finely chopped green cabbage, one quart of chopped cucumbers, one quart of sweet green peppers, chopped, and a few white radishes, chopped. Place the vegetables in a stone jar, and pour over them enough cold water to cover, to which has been added one cupful of salt. Let stand overnight, and the next day drain off the salty water. Put three quarts of vinegar in a porcelain-lined kettle, add three cupfuls of sugar, and little bags of cheese-cloth containing the following spices: one ounce each of allspice, cloves, mace, pepper, mustard and celery seed, or if preferred mixed spices can be used. Put in the vegetables, and boil until tender; if there is not enough vinegar to cover the vegetables add a little more, also a little salt if it is not salty enough. Put into jars and seal.

A White Relish

The white relish is made by using one gallon of the inner white leaves of cabbage chopped quite fine, one quart of white celery, chopped into bits, one quart of white, stringless pod beans cut into bits, and one quart of chopped silver-skinned onions. Sprinkle all the vegetables except the onions with salt, using about a cupful; cover with cold water, and let stand overnight. In the morning drain off the cold water, place the vegetables in a kettle, adding the chopped onions, one cupful of grated horseradish, one ounce of celery seed, one ounce of white mustard seed, three cupfuls of granulated sugar, and a little white ginger root. Cover with good, clear vinegar, and cook until the vegetables are tender; then put into jars and seal. A little more salt may be added before jars are sealed.

Tomato Catsup

To make good tomato catsup, take one peck of ripe, firm, red tomatoes, cut out the stem ends, slice and then hash. Add three tablespoonfuls of salt, and boil in a porcelain-lined kettle until soft; then pass through a fine sieve, put back on the stove, and add one teaspoonful of cayenne pepper, one tablespoonful each of ground black pepper, cloves and mace, and four tablespoonfuls of ground mustard. A few bay leaves may be added, or a tablespoonful of celery seed tied up in a bag. Boil slowly for about four hours, stirring often; let stand overnight, then add a pint of good clear cider vinegar. Bring to a boil, put into bottles, and seal while hot.

Ripe Tomato Catsup

Take two pecks of ripe tomatoes, one pound of brown sugar, one-half dozen of medium-sized onions, one-quarter of a pound of allspice, one-quarter of a pound of green peppers, one-quarter of a pound of whole cloves, one quart of good cider vinegar, one-half teaspoonful of cayenne pepper, and salt.

Scald and peel the tomatoes; place in a kettle with the onions, sliced; add the spices and simmer slowly until the onions are tender, stirring to prevent burning. Rub the pulp through a sieve or colander and place in the kettle again; boil to the consistency of catsup. Add salt to taste. Put in bottles and seal. This makes a very toothsome catsup. If you wish a milder catsup, omit part of the pepper, and cut down the amount of the other spices.

Cinnamon and mace may be added.

Tomato-Pepper Relish

Take one gallon of ripe tomatoes, one-half dozen of medium-sized onions, one quart of cider vinegar, one ounce of celery seed, one tablespoonful of ground cinnamon, one-half dozen red peppers, one teaspoonful of ground mustard, three green peppers, one cupful of brown sugar, one-half teaspoonful of cayenne, one teaspoonful of whole pepper, and salt.

Scald and peel the tomatoes. Chop the onions and peppers, removing seeds from the latter, and add to the tomatoes. Add the vinegar, sugar, and spices, and simmer slowly until onions and peppers are tender. Pass through a colander, and boil to the consistency of a sauce. The sauce is good if it is not passed through a colander.

HORSERADISH CATSUP

To a quart of grated horseradish add the following mixture, previously well blended together. One cupful each of cider vinegar and olive oil, one teaspoonful of salt, one-fourth cupful of granulated sugar, one tablespoonful of mustard, a quarter of a teaspoonful of pepper, and if desired a little grated onion. Fill jars or bottles, and seal tight.

MUSHROOM CATSUP

Place the mushrooms in a preserving kettle or earthen vessel, sprinkling each layer with salt. Allow them to stand overnight, then in the morning crush with a wooden spoon, or better, pass through a fine sieve. Add to each quart of the mushrooms three small red peppercorns, a half dozen cloves, a bay leaf, one stick of cinnamon, and a bit of mace. Boil until thick; then thin down to the consistency of catsup with strong vinegar, and seal in bottles or jars.

Onion Catsup

Arrange equal quantities of sliced onion, green sliced tomatoes and apples in alternate layers in an earthenware vessel, sprinkling salt liberally between layers, using about a tablespoonful to each three pounds of the mixture. Allow to stand overnight, then drain. Pass them through the fine cutter of the food chopper. Put them in a preserving kettle and add enough vinegar to cover, add spices and let simmer slowly until ingredients are cooked, and the consistency of catsup.

The apples may be omitted, and only onions and tomatoes used. Ripe tomatoes may be used instead of green if preferred.

IX

Miscellaneous

CHAPTER IX

MISCELLANEOUS

CANDIED FRUITS AND FLOWERS

NEARLY all kinds of fruits may be candied; but the ones that have proved the most satisfactory to me are cherries, strawberries, pineapple, peaches, pears, currants, and gooseberries. Mint and other aromatic leaves are fine candied, and among the flowers I find rose petals and violets best suited to this purpose.

CANDIED CHERRIES

In making candied cherries I use the large red cherries. Boiling water is poured over them after the stones have been removed; they are allowed to stand in this a while, then the water is poured off, and the cherries drained. In a preserving kettle is placed a pound and a half of sugar and one-half cupful of water to each pound of fruit. This is boiled to the soft-ball stage; then the cherries are added, and simmered very slowly for fifteen or twenty minutes or until the cherries are red and transparent; then they are removed with a skimmer, and placed on platters. These are placed in the strong sun, or in a slow oven until nearly dry. The syrup in the kettle is cooked down to the hard-ball stage and a little red fruit coloring added; then the cherries are placed in this a few at a time, and simmered slowly until each cherry is well permeated with the syrup; then they are removed to the platter again, and placed in the sun until thoroughly dried; they are then packed in pasteboard boxes or tins lined with paraffin paper.

Paraffin paper is also placed between each two layers.

Strawberries and Other Fruits

The strawberries are candied in the same way, only instead of pouring boiling water over them they are placed in a preserving kettle with the sugar in alternate layers, and allowed to stand overnight; then the juice is poured off into a preserving kettle, and brought to the soft-ball stage, and the berries added, a few at a time, and the same process gone through as with the cherries. The pineapple is cut up in about inch slices, then cut into cubes, or fourths. Proceed as for candied cherries.

The largest gooseberries are used for candying, and when green. The stems are removed, they are cut lengthwise, and the seeds picked out, using the point of a small fruit knife.

When candying peaches and pears, especially pears, a little lemon rind or ginger root is often added to the syrup; or a little vanilla or almond extract. If the fruit is to be crystallized I boil down the syrup to the crystal state, and pour this over the fruit on the platters, and let stand until the crystals are dry.

Leaves and Flowers

Leaves and flowers are a little more difficult to candy, as they cannot stand much handling. I use a pound of sugar to each pint of leaves, and just enough water to dissolve it. The leaves are laid out singly on platters or tins. The sugar is boiled to the soft-ball stage; then with a spoon the syrup is dipped over the leaves, which are allowed to stand overnight. The syrup is then drained from the leaves by placing them on a sieve. The syrup is boiled to the candy stage, then dipped over the leaves as before, and again let stand for several hours. If by that time crystals are not formed over the leaves this is repeated once more; then let stand until dry, which may be hastened by placing them in the hot sun for a while. Place the leaves in single rows between sheets of waxed paper, and pack in boxes. The flowers may be candied in the same manner.

Candied fruits should always be stored in a cool place.

CANDIED PEACHES

Choose large ripe but firm peaches for this purpose. Peel, and halve. Make a thick syrup with granulated sugar and water, using a cupful of water to each pound of sugar. Place the peaches in this and bring to a boil. Simmer for about five minutes; then remove from fire, and let stand overnight in the syrup. Place over the fire again, and allow the peaches to simmer another five minutes. Skim carefully out on to platters, and place in the sun or in a slow oven until dry. Again bring the syrup to a boil, add the peaches and simmer to the crystal state, then remove the peaches on to platters again, and let dry as before. Before they are quite dry, sprinkle with chopped almonds, or the kernels of the peach-stones can be chopped and used. When completely dry, pack in boxes lined with paraffin-paper, and place a sheet of paper between each two layers. Pears and pineapples may be candied in the same manner.

TOMATO FIGS

These are fine, and are as easily made as the candied fruits and flowers. The small yellow to-matoes are the best for this purpose. They should be ripe but firm. Wipe the tomatoes off, and then arrange in alternate layers in a preserving kettle with granulated sugar, using an equal quantity of fruit and sugar. Allow to stand for at least twenty-four hours. Place the kettle in the oven a few minutes to melt any of the sugar not yet melted; then drain off the juice into another preserving kettle. Add about an ounce of ginger root and the yellow rind and juice of three lemons for each gallon of tomatoes.

Boil to a thick syrup; then add the tomatoes, a few at a time, and simmer until transparent. Remove carefully to platters with a skimmer, and place in the sun, carefully protecting from dust and insects with fine netting or coarse cheese-cloth, using a frame to place it over so that it will not touch the fruit. After the "figs" have been in the sun for several days place the syrup over the fire and boil to the candy stage, then dip each fig into this, then place them in the sun or in a moderate oven until thoroughly dry. Pack like candied fruits.

STRAWBERRIES FOR WINTER SHORTCAKES

One may have uncooked strawberries for shortcakes and frozen desserts in the winter by putting up the strawberries in the following manner:

Rub the firm, ripe berries through a sieve fine enough to retain the seeds. Measure the pulp, and to each pint add one pound of sugar. Stir until the sugar has permeated all the pulp—to be sure of this it is best to stir about half an hour. Fill into pint jars about two-thirds full, or within two inches of the top. Have equal parts of currant juice and sugar on the stove and boil to a thick jelly. Pour this over the strawberry pulp. When cold cover with a layer of sugar, and pour over this melted paraffin and screw on the lids.

QUINCE HONEY

Choose for this honey nice ripe quinces, pare, core and grate. To a pint of the grated fruit allow three pounds of sugar and a pint of water.

Boil the sugar and water until it spins a thread, add the grated quince and boil until as thick as honey. Pour into jars and seal while hot. This is good to serve with hot breads and cakes in the winter.

PEACH HONEY

Take any peaches as you would for making jelly, or you need only use the skins and pits which are discarded when making preserves. Add plenty of water to cover and simmer slowly for at least a half hour. Drain off the juice into a vessel, and use as much sugar as juice. Boil to the consistency of honey, and fill into bottles or screw-top jars and seal while hot. This is excellent to use in making sauces for puddings, as a syrup for pancakes, or to eat with bread and butter, like any other honey.

VEGETABLE JAMS AND JELLIES

Very few people think of using vegetables for making preserves and jellies, yet very good results may be had with carrots, beets and tomatoes. The best results are obtained with vegetables by combining them with fruits.

BEET JELLY

Take young tender beets, and wash very thoroughly, and boil in enough water to cover until tender. Mash, and place in a jelly bag, and let drain. To each cupful of this beet juice add a cupful of rhubarb juice, and to each pint of juice add three-fourths of a pound of granulated sugar. Boil as you would in making other jelly, and add the sugar when hot, and cook until it jellies, and you will have a nice pink jelly to fill into jelly glasses.

CARROT CONSERVE

Use the deep, orange carrots for this; clean and scrape, and cook until tender and pass through the fine cutter of a food chopper. To each pint of this carrot pulp add one pound of sugar, and the outside rind and juice of two oranges, and one lemon.

Add a little water, then cook very slowly until you have a thick conserve or marmalade.

GREEN TOMATO JAM

Take equal quantities of green tomatoes and green grapes. Slice the tomatoes, and add the grapes, and enough water to cover. Boil slowly until tender, then pass through a colander or coarse sieve. To each pint of the pulp add a pound of sugar, and boil down to the consistency of jam, and fill into glasses or jars.

TOMATO-PEACH JAM

Use the small yellow tomatoes for this jam. Use equal quantities of tomatoes and yellow peaches. Cook slowly until tender, then pass through a colander or coarse sieve. Place in a preserving kettle after measuring the pulp, and to each pint add a pound of sugar. Boil to the consistency of jam. If liked this may be flavored with a little lemon rind or vanilla.

Tomato Conserve

Use green or partly ripe tomatoes, and to each peck of tomatoes use about two pounds of seedless or seeded raisins, five pounds of brown sugar, and one teaspoonful of cinnamon, and one-half teaspoonful of ground cloves or allspice. Cook the tomatoes and raisins until soft, then add the sugar and spices, and boil to the thickness of conserves. If liked a few tart apples may be added.

Index

165

POPULAR· HAND-BOOKS

SOME books are designed for entertainment, others for information. ¶ This series combines both features. The information is not only complete and reliable, it is compact and readable. In this busy, bustling age it is required that the information which books contain shall be ready to hand and be presented in the clearest and briefest manner possible. ¶ These volumes are replete with valuable information, compact in form and unequalled in point of merit and cheapness. They are the latest as well as the best books on the subjects of which they treat. No one who wishes to have a fund of general information or who has the desire for self-improvement can afford to be without them. ¶ They are 6 x 4½ inches in size, well printed on good paper, handsomely bound in green cloth, with a heavy paper wrapper to match.

Cloth, each 50 cents

THE PENN PUBLISHING COMPANY
925 Filbert St., Philadelphia

ETIQUETTE
By Agnes H. Morton

There is no passport to good society like good manners. ¶ Even though one possess wealth and intelligence, his success in life may be marred by ignorance of social customs. ¶ A perusal of this book will prevent such blunders. It is a book for everybody, for the social leaders as well as for those less ambitious. ¶ The subject is presented in a bright and interesting manner, and represents the latest vogue.

LETTER WRITING
By Agnes H. Morton

Why do most persons dislike to write letters? Is it not because they cannot say the right thing in the right place? This admirable book not only shows by numerous examples just what kind of letters to write, but by directions and suggestions enables the reader to become an accomplished original letter writer. ¶ There are forms for all kinds of business and social letters, including invitations, acceptances, letters of sympathy, congratulations, and love letters.

QUOTATIONS
By Agnes H. Morton

A clever compilation of pithy quotations, selected from a great variety of sources, and alphabetically arranged according to the sentiment. ¶ In addition to all the popular quotations in current use, it contains many rare bits of prose and verse not generally found in similar collections. ¶ One important feature of the book is found in the characteristic lines from well known authors, in which the familiar sayings are credited to their original sources.

EPITAPHS
By Frederic W. Unger

Even death has its humorous side. ¶ There are said to be "sermons in stones," but when they are tombstones there is many a smile mixed with the moral. ¶ Usually churchyard humor is all the more delightful because it is unconscious, but there are times when it is intentional and none the less amusing. ¶ Of epitaphs, old and new, this book contains the best. It is full of quaint bits of obituary fancy, with a touch of the gruesome here and there for a relish.

PROVERBS
By John H. Bechtel

The genius, wit, and spirit of a nation are discovered in its proverbs, and the condensed wisdom of all ages and all nations is embodied in them. ¶ A good proverb that fits the case is often a convincing argument. ¶ This volume contains a representative collection of proverbs, old and new, and the indexes, topical and alphabetical, enable one to find readily just what he requires.

THINGS WORTH KNOWING
By John H. Bechtel

Can you name the coldest place in the United States or tell what year had 445 days? Do you know how soon the coal fields of the world are likely to be exhausted, or how the speed of a moving train may be told? What should you do first if you got a cinder in your eye, or your neighbor's baby swallowed a pin? This unique, up-to-date book answers thousands of just such interesting and useful questions.

A DICTIONARY OF MYTHOLOGY

By John H. Bechtel

Most of us dislike to look up a mythological subject because of the time required. ¶ This book remedies that difficulty because in it can be found at a glance just what is wanted. ¶ It is comprehensive, convenient, condensed, and the information is presented in such an interesting manner that when once read it will always be remembered. ¶ A distinctive feature of the book is the pronunciation of the proper names, something found in few other works.

SLIPS OF SPEECH

By John H. Bechtel

Who does not make them? The best of us do. ¶ Why not avoid them? Any one inspired with the spirit of self-improvement may readily do so. ¶ No necessity for studying rules of grammar or rhetoric when this book may be had. It teaches both without the study of either. ¶ It is a counsellor, a critic, a companion, and a guide, and is written in a most entertaining and chatty style.

HANDBOOK OF PRONUNCIATION

By John H. Bechtel

What is more disagreeable than a faulty pronunciation? No other defect so clearly shows a lack of culture. ¶ This book contains over 5,000 words on which most of us are apt to trip. ¶ They are here pronounced in the clearest and simplest manner, and according to the best authority ¶ It is more readily consulted than a dictionary, and is just as reliable.

PRACTICAL SYNONYMS
By John H. Bechtel

A new word is a new tool. ¶ This book will not only enlarge your vocabulary, but will show you how to express the exact shade of meaning you have in mind, and will cultivate a more precise habit of thought and speech. ¶ It will be found invaluable to busy journalists, merchants, lawyers, or clergymen, and as an aid to teachers no less than to the boys and girls under their care.

READY MADE SPEECHES
By George Hapgood, Esq.

Pretty much everybody in these latter days, is now and again called upon "to say a few words in public." ¶ Unfortunately, however, but few of us are gifted with the power of ready and graceful speech. ¶ This is a book of carefully planned model speeches to aid those who, without some slight help, must remain silent. ¶ There is a preliminary chapter of general advice to speakers.

AFTER-DINNER STORIES
By John Harrison

The dinner itself may be ever so good, and yet prove a failure if there is no mirth to enliven the company. ¶ Nothing adds so much zest to an occasion of this kind as a good story well told. ¶ Here are hundreds of the latest, best, brightest, and most catchy stories, all of them short and pithy, and so easy to remember that anyone can tell them successfully. ¶ There are also a number of selected toasts suitable to all occasions.

TOASTS

By William Pittenger

Most men dread being called upon to respond to a toast or to make an address. ¶ What would you not give for the ability to be rid of this embarrassment? No need to give much when you can learn the art from this little book. ¶ It will tell you how to do it; not only that, but by example it will show the way. ¶ It is valuable not alone to the novice, but to the experienced speaker, who will gather from it many suggestions.

THE DEBATER'S TREASURY

By William Pittenger

There is no greater ability than the power of skillful and forcible debate, and no accomplishment more readily acquired if the person is properly directed. ¶ In this little volume are directions for organizing and conducting debating societies and practical suggestions for all who desire to discuss questions in public. ¶ There is also a list of over 200 questions for debate, with arguments both affirmative and negative.

PUNCTUATION

By Paul Allardyce

Few persons can punctuate properly; to avoid mistakes many do not punctuate at all. ¶ A perusal of this book will remove all difficulties and make all points clear. ¶ The rules are plainly stated and freely illustrated, thus furnishing a most useful volume. ¶ The author is everywhere recognized as the leading authority upon the subject, and what he has to say is practical, concise, and comprehensive.

CANDY-MAKING AT HOME
By Mary M. Wright

Two hundred ways to make candy with the home flavor and the professional finish. ¶ Clear and detailed recipes are given for fondant, fruit and nut candies, cream candies, fudges and caramels, bonbons, macaroons and little cakes. ¶ Every housekeeper can now greatly lessen the cost of entertainments by preparing at home the confectionery to be used and can also keep her table well supplied with delicious bonbons and candies

THE CARE OF THE CHILD
By Mrs. Burton Chance

One of the few books that deal with this old and ever ·new problem in all its aspects —mental, moral and physical. ¶ The author, a mother and the wife of a physician, has anticipated nearly every nursery difficulty. ¶ She gives all that one ordinarily needs about diet, clothing, bathing and sleep, summarizing the practice of leading specialists. ¶ There are helpful practical discussions on obedience, imagination, personality, truthtelling, play and education.

HOME DECORATION
By Dorothy T. Priestman

A beautiful home means only knowing what to buy when you do buy. ¶ This is a book that tells what is really in simple good taste, why, and how to get it. ¶ It deals fully and practically with the treatment of walls, furniture, floor covering, hangings, ornaments and pictures. ¶ It gives color schemes, tells how to arrange a door or a window; how to make the most of small space; how to do stenciling; how to make rugs, etc.

THE FAMILY FOOD
By T. C. O'Donnell

Most of us eat too much. ¶ All of us pay more than we need for our food. ¶ A practical, thorough book on the way to get the most efficient food for little money. ¶ It discusses every familiar article of diet, tells its cost, its food value, and its effects on the body, and gives menus showing how to economize and keep well. ¶ It is written in a simple plain style for plain people, by a recognized authority.

THE FAMILY HEALTH
By Myer Solis-Cohen, M.D.

This book tells how to keep well, and how to build up the natural forces that combat disease. ¶ It gives definite information that can be put into practice. ¶ It treats problems of ventilation, heating, lighting, drainage, disposal of refuse, destruction of insects, and cleansing. ¶ Under personal hygiene it discusses bathing, clothing, food, drink, work, exercise, rest and the care of the eyes, ears, throat, teeth, nails, hair and figure. ¶ A chapter is devoted to the mind, and the prevention of nervousness and insanity. ¶ Directions are given for nursing at home. ¶ This book tells the family just "what to do before the doctor arrives."

THE FAMILY HOUSE
By C. F. Osborne, Architect

A helpful book that tells what to look for in the location of a house, price or amount of rent, exposure, plumbing, fixtures, lighting, ventilation, water, how to tell whether a house is well built, dry and warm, what is the best plan and how to get comfort and artistic effects in furnishing. ¶ Whether one is renting, buying or building, this book will save annoyance, time and money.